ADDENDUM

This second printing of *Long Island Landmarks* has been made possible by a grant from the New York State Council on the Arts' Museum Aid Program to the Society for the Preservation of Long Island Antiquities. Only minor typographic corrections have been made in the text to permit rapid reprinting and distribution.

The original printing of 8,000 copies was exhausted within two months after its release by the State Office of Planning Coordination in January 1970. Publicity about the book and related articles on significant structures and areas have sparked new and renewed interest in architectural and historic preservation, resulting in a steady stream of requests for this book.

When it became known that the original stock was depleted, the Society for the Preservation of Long Island Antiquities, aware of the value of this publication, was pleased to cooperate in making a second printing available as a public service.

Long Island Landmarks is by no means an all-inclusive listing of distinctive structures. It is hoped, however, that it will serve as a model for more extensive preservation studies by groups on Long Island and in other sections of the state. Several landmarks pictured or mentioned have already been demolished or are in imminent danger of destruction, indicating a need for prompt action by both public official and private citizen in implementing appropriate programs for preservation outlined in Part III, page 86.

The Society is providing the State Office of Planning Services, the successor agency of the Office of Planning Coordination, with sufficient copies to fill requests received since the original supply was exhausted. Future requests should be addressed to:

> The Society for the Preservation of
>   Long Island Antiquities
> North Country Road, Box 206
> Setauket, Long Island, New York 11733.

Contents

PART I *Introduction* 4
    The Setting 5
    The History 5
        Colonial Period (1640 to 1730) 6
        Georgian Period (1730 to 1790) 7
        Federal Period (1790 to 1830) 8
        Greek Revival Period (1830 to 1860) 9
        Victorian Period (1845 to 1880) 9
        Eclectic Period (1880 to date) 11
    The Problem 12
PART II *Architectural Landmarks* 13
    Town of Hempstead 14
        Village of Freeport Area 16
        Garden City Area 16
    Town of North Hempstead 20
        Roslyn Area 22
    Town of Oyster Bay 26
        Old Bethpage Village Restoration Area 28
        Sea Cliff Area 28
    Town of Babylon 30
        Amityville Area 31
        Babylon Area 33
    Town of Brookhaven 34
        Bellport Area 35
        Center Moriches-East Moriches Area 37
        Mount Sinai-Miller Place Area 37
        Port Jefferson Area 39
        Setauket, East Setauket, Stony Brook, Old Field Area 40
    Town of East Hampton 42
        Route 27 Area 43
    Town of Huntington 46
        Cold Spring Harbor Area 48
        Huntington Area 51
        Melville Area 51
    Town of Islip 52
    Town of Riverhead 56
        Route 25 Area 58

Town of Shelter Island	60
Town of Smithtown	64
Fort Salonga Area	65
Route 25A Area	66
Village of the Branch Area	67
Town of Southampton	70
Bridgehampton Area	71
Sagaponack Area	72
Sag Harbor Area	73
Southampton Area	77
Town of Southold	78
Route 25	80
Greenport Area	82
Orient Area	83
PART III *Programs for Preservation*	86
Comprehensive Program	87
Private Sector	88
Historic Societies	89
Preservation Corporations	89
Gifts	90
Lending Institutions	90
Public Sector	91
Acquisition	91
Preservation, Historic District and Aesthetic Zoning Legislation	93
Landmarks Preservation Commission	94
Survey and Designation	95
Comprehensive Planning Program	95
Zoning and Subdivision Controls	96
Conclusion	96
APPENDIX: *Architectural Landmark Evaluation and Index*	97
Areas	100
Nassau	100
Suffolk	100
Structures	104
Nassau	104
Suffolk	109

Part I

Introduction

THE SETTING

Now more than ever before, Americans are expressing concern about their past. The magnitude and rapidity of change, and the complexities of modern society which contribute to or necessitate change make us more aware of our origins and heritage.

This awareness has taken many forms: the emphasis on conservation of unique natural resources, the resurgent interest in antiques for their beauty and image of the past, the restoration of entire communities to capture at one point in time the way in which Americans of other eras lived and worked.

Another aspect of this growing awareness of the past is the preservation of our architectural landmarks, individual structures or small concentrations. Every building has an architectural character, some have an historical connection with famous persons or events, and a few have both. All have the potential to contribute pleasure, knowledge and a sense of continuity and of history. The challenge and responsibility which every generation faces is to identify, select and preserve those of the greatest significance — a difficult task under the constraints of time and money. More frequently than not these work against the preservation of worthwhile structures, particularly in areas of rapid growth where the competition for space spirals land values upwards. Such an area is Long Island.

This then is the focus of this study — to identify the buildings in Nassau and Suffolk Counties which deserve preservation for their quality, uniqueness or history; to evaluate their present status; and to discuss available resources and techniques for architectural and historic preservation.

Preservation is not an accident. It requires deliberate, conscious choice. This volume will help to make that choice in favor of preserving Long Island's landmarks.

THE HISTORY

Despite its proximity to New York City, Long Island was a slow-growing agricultural area, generally conservative culturally. Because architecture evolved gradually, a particular style is often reflected in buildings dated well after the style has phased out elsewhere. Nor was it a wealthy area; its architecture, with few sophisticated buildings, reflects the life of average citizens.

Although Nassau and Suffolk Counties are among the oldest settled areas in New York State, they have considerable

Medieval

modern development. The blending of old architecture with new and the tremendous scenic and recreational influences of its shoreline, provide variety and charm for residents and visitors.

This very combination of the old and the rapidly changing new highlights the major problems in preservation. In 1885, a writer in *Harper's New Monthly Magazine* lamented the changes in Suffolk's eastern tips: "two landmarks of the past have disappeared — and more's the pity."

Old House, Cutchogue

Growth since 1900 has destroyed many landmarks, replacing them with commercial buildings and suburban housing developments. Continuing growth brings massive developments and other changes which threaten remaining landmarks.

Basically, Long Island architecture follows American architectural history. The following sections indicate the generally accepted divisions, noting special Long Island characteristics, but style periods are somewhat arbitrary, particularly in nomenclature and time designation.

Salt Box

Colonial Period (1640 to 1730)

The great diversity of Long Island's architecture traces to its settlement in the 1640s. English settlers from New England occupied the island from the Town of

John Payne House, East Hampton

Dutch House

Hempstead eastward through the two forks, while Dutch settlers spread into the Towns of Hempstead and Oyster Bay.

Until 1730, the major influence came from English architecture. Original homes were medieval in feeling — like the Old House at Cutchogue, with steep roofs, large outer chimneys and windows with small leaded panes. Early New England influence was also widespread, with many saltbox and Cape Cod houses, particularly along the North Shore. Dutch influence is seen in buildings such as the Cooper House at the Old Bethpage Village restoration, with its Flemish sweeping curved roof eave extending several feet beyond the house front, and the still-popular Dutch doorway.

Cooper House, Old Bethpage Village

As in later periods, wood was the major construction material and massive hewn oak beams continued until the early 1800s. Before 1900, brick or stone houses were rare on Long Island and only a few pre-Civil War ones still remain. Rubble stone, however, was used for foundations and for the immense end-wall fireplaces in Dutch houses.

Georgian

Georgian Period (1730 to 1790)

The more formal Georgian style, based on symmetrical design, offered balanced facades, with paneled front doorways leading to wide entrance halls and

Rock Hall, Lawrence

7

center stairways. Sash windows were introduced, first with 24 panes but gradually with fewer panes later in the period. Exteriors were almost exclusively shingle on Long Island, and buildings before 1750 used long, rounded end butts of up to 36 inches. Columns, pilasters and pediments were rare.

Federal

The gambrel roof was popular during this era. A fine example, with the typical roof deck, is on Rock Hall in Lawrence, one of the best Georgian buildings in the United States. Cupolas in the center of the roof continued as a feature through the mid-1800s. Interior paneling based on classical forms was frequent and fireplaces had borders of Dutch tiles.

Federal Period (1790 to 1830)

The Federal period continued the classical qualities of the Georgian period, refining and intensifying the classical nature of the building. Giant porticos with Doric columns became common, and the entrance doorway with narrow leaded sidelights and half-circle fanlight became a central feature. Exteriors were still normally shingle, but clapboard siding was in use by the end of the period. Matching end chimneys were common and many earlier homes were remodeled to include them.

Interiors echoed the classical theme,

Sylvester Manor, Shelter Island

8

Greek Revival

with carved wood or molded plaster trim and room ornaments, graceful spiral stairways and simple painted plaster walls, normally left white on Long Island.

Greek Revival Period (1830 to 1860)

Classical influence reached its height in the Greek Revival period, shown in entire buildings or only in a small portico over the entrance. Hallmarks are broad flat surfaces and monumental white porticos, following the traditional Greek, Doric, Ionic and Corinthian orders, with a low triangular pediment — as in the Onderdonk House in Manhasset. The design was frequently asymetrical; many typical Long Island "half-houses" had the main doorway on one side of the block. Exterior treatment now was usually clapboard siding.

Victorian Period (1845 to 1880)

During the Victorian period architecture reflected the general national interest in, and admiration for, foreign cultures, and various phases and forms showed direct European influence. Two prominent influences on Long Island were the Gothic Revival (1845 to 1870) and French (1860 to 1880).

Gothic design added an exotic touch to even simple house architecture with towers, balconies and wings added at will.

Onderdonk House, Manhasset

9

Victorian

Victorian House, Lloyd Harbor

Carpenter Gothic

Swiss House, Sea Cliff

Queen Anne

Sagamore Hill, Cove Neck

The mansard roof was the principal sign of French influence; arched windows and delicate iron railings crowning the roof contrasted sharply with existing and traditional styles. As elsewhere in the United States, many structures duplicated the Italianate style, using bracketed cornices and high square towers. Simple versions combined these influences, along with many plain carpenter-style and gingerbread houses in the late 19th century.

Eclectic Period (1880 to date)

By the late 1880s, the new movement of using style idioms from all over the world began to affect Long Island. Queen Anne houses, reminiscent of Tudor manor houses, began to spread over wooded plots. With the rise of the Gold Coast from 1890 to 1930, multi-million dollar estates introduced every conceivable style — from exact reproductions of Georgian brick manorial homes (the Phipps House in Old Westbury) to Irish stone castles (the Guggenheim estate in Sands Point).

Long Island architecture turned full circle after World War II when Levittown added thousands of Cape Cod homes to the Hempstead plains. Contemporary architecture is extremely varied, from a small Frank Lloyd Wright home at Great Neck to distinctive beach houses by today's young architects along Suffolk County South Fork in the Towns of Southampton and East Hampton.

11

Phipps House, Old Westbury

Frank Lloyd Wright House, Great Neck

THE PROBLEM

Long Island's rapidly growing population of more than 2.5 million in several hundred communities, and its 1,200-square-mile area, create very different geographical problems for landmark preservation. While there is no single method for preserving every structure, all the landmarks of Long Island share many problems.

Costs of preservation are higher than elsewhere in the United States and compete with other urgent needs. Both counties have very high real estate taxes and most landmarks are on main routes where property values are highest. Increasing taxation and rising land values create pressures on owners to redevelop their property economically, and this usually means demolition.

Local, state and federal public works continually threaten and demolish structures, particularly for new or widened highways. Long Island's needs for improvements and plans for bridges across Long Island Sound to Connecticut increase the threat. Nassau County has lost many of its best landmarks to this process and Suffolk County is beginning to experience this impact.

Detailed, well-researched information on architectural landmarks, essential to any adequate plan for preservation, is greatly lacking in this region. Since the Historic American Buildings Survey recorded 51 Long Island buildings in the 1930s, individuals and organizations have done only sporadic survey work. Because information varies in quality and little raw data has been published, the information is difficult to locate and usually requires original research.

Where buildings have been saved, a major problem of maintenance and preservation remains. Information on these techniques is lacking and many landmarks are deteriorating because maintenance is inadequate.

Only careful planning can save many structures which contribute so significantly to the environment and which attract so many people to Nassau and Suffolk Counties and this planning requires the determined efforts of individuals, businesses, private organizations, institutions, historical societies and every level of government.

Implementation also requires the collaboration of all.

Part II

Architectural Landmarks

This discussion of architectural and historic landmarks is not exhaustive, but focuses on two categories: concentrations of landmarks within a small geographic section, designated as "areas"; and individual buildings which are threatened. A more comprehensive listing of landmark buildings and areas is in the appendix.

Areas and buildings are arranged by town. A map in each section shows their general location within the town and photographs illustrate the landmarks mentioned.

Most are residences, because these have had the greatest survival power, but churches, commercial districts, industrial structures, farm buildings and even a railroad station are also discussed. Almost all these landmarks were built before the 20th century.

Hempstead

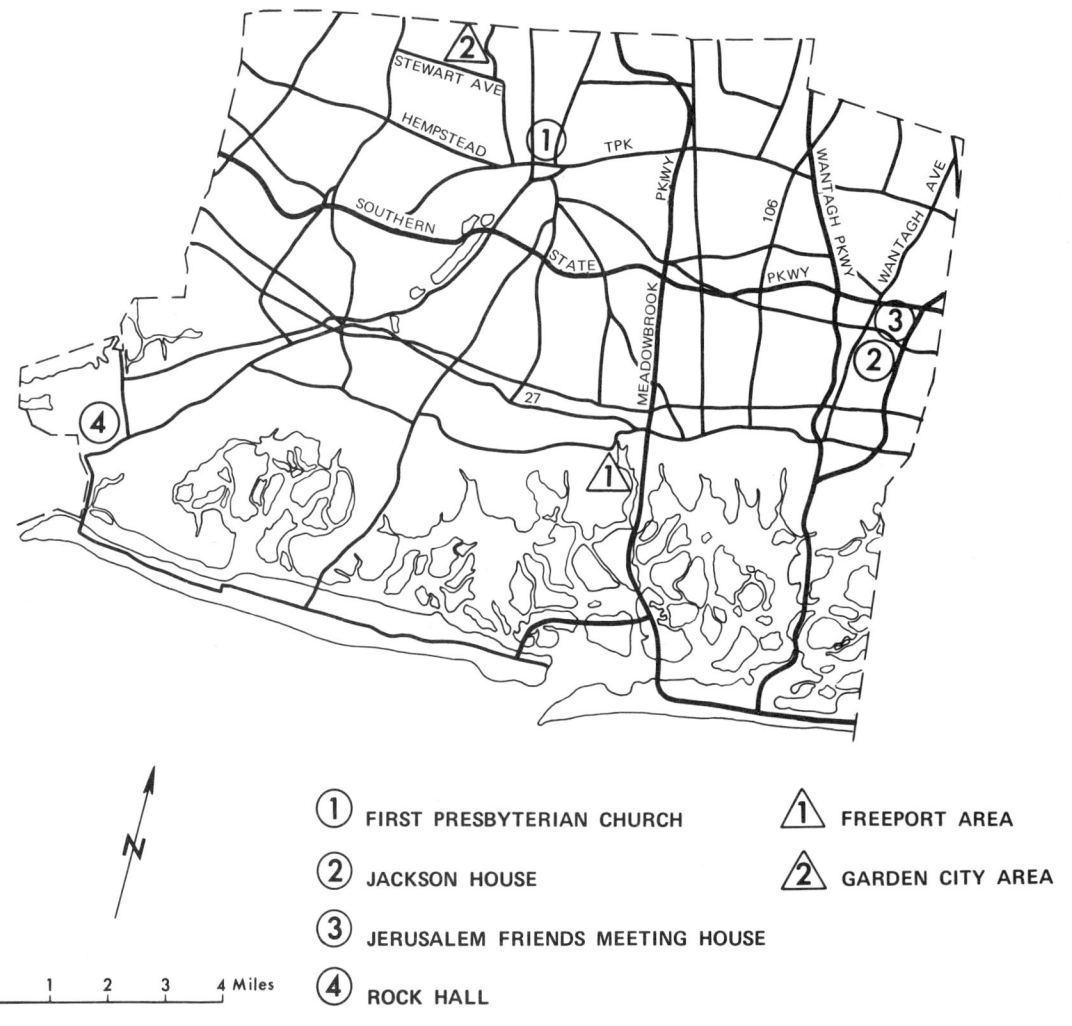

① FIRST PRESBYTERIAN CHURCH
② JACKSON HOUSE
③ JERUSALEM FRIENDS MEETING HOUSE
④ ROCK HALL

△1 FREEPORT AREA
△2 GARDEN CITY AREA

TOWN OF HEMPSTEAD

Hempstead is the largest town in Nassau County, with an area of 143 square miles and a population of 832,000 in one city, 21 villages and many unincorporated communities. Scattered structures reflecting its history back to 1644 are of architectural note within what is now bustling suburbia.

The First Presbyterian Church in Hempstead, erected in 1846, is one of the few remaining public pre-1860 structures and an exceptional example of Gothic influence in American architecture. Its future is uncertain because of the congregation's move to a new church.

First Presbyterian Church, Hempstead

The Jackson House on Wantagh Avenue in Wantagh is a good example of a Long Island farmhouse as it developed through the years. Nearby, the Jerusalem Friends Meeting House is one of the few such remaining structures from the early 1800s, although continued modification is compromising its simple architectural style.

One of the last great manor houses still remaining on Long Island is Rock Hall, in Lawrence. It is nationally recognized as a foremost example of colonial Georgian architecture, and is now excellently cared for by the Town of Hempstead.

Jackson House, Wantagh

Jerusalem Friends Meeting House, Wantagh

Rock Hall, Lawrence

Gingerbread House, Freeport

Village of Freeport Area

The waterfront past of the village of Freeport is glimpsed in a small area on South Main Street, particularly in the gingerbread house at the old Oyster Wharf and several Victorian structures nearby. Property values are high but the area is threatened.

Garden City Area

A. T. Stewart, a wealthy drygoods merchant, bought a large share of the Town of Hempstead common lands after the Civil War for creating an ideal community. Garden City was to be the village of the future, with spacious roads, green vistas and high quality homes. The initial development around the railroad station still contains a remarkable number of 1870 to 1900 structures — not ordinary late Victorian homes, but stately houses that set the tone for Garden City's development as one of Long Island's exclusive villages. Early structures built by Stewart interests include matching groups of Apostle and Disciple homes. These mansard roof homes and other Victorian structures in the village are in great demand, rare resales bring high prices and the homes seem reasonably secure.

The Cathedral of the Incarnation, which Stewart's widow built in his memory in 1883, is one of the nation's best reproductions of 13th century Gothic architec-

Victorian House, Garden City

Cathedral of the Incarnation, Garden City

Garden City Hotel, Garden City

ture, with a majestic floriated 220-foot spire of pink sandstone. The nearby Garden City Hotel, designed by the noted firm of McKim, Mead and White, was built in 1900 to replace an earlier hotel. The four-story Georgian Revival building, a favorite of America's elite throughout the early 1900s, has been the island's most famous hotel. It occupies a large, key piece of land, and the Village of Garden City has resisted rezoning to further develop the property. The success of a new owner, who has undertaken extensive renovation, is crucial to the building's future and to its significant contribution to the environment in the village's core.

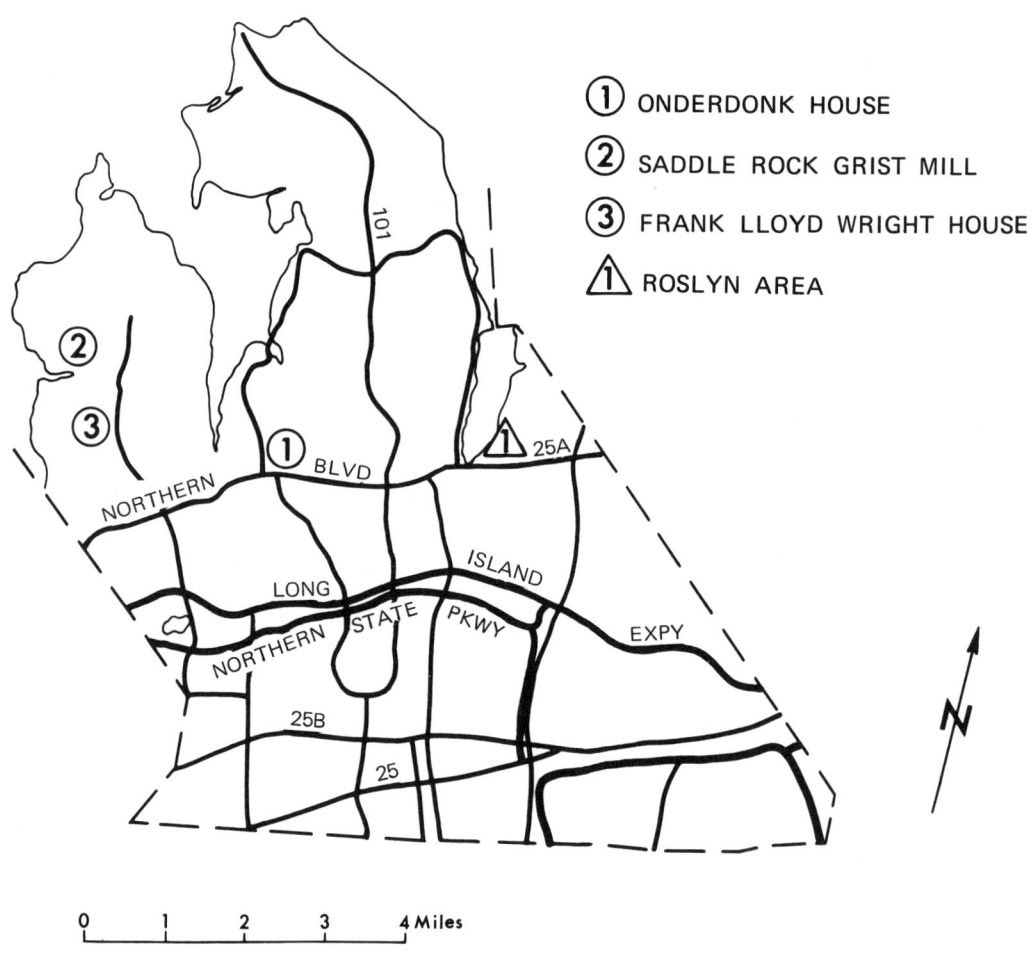

Grist Mill, Saddle Rock

TOWN OF NORTH HEMPSTEAD

Most of North Hempstead's 54 square miles is divided among one city and 30 villages; the population is over 240,000. The town is rich in contemporary buildings, including several Gold Coast mansions from the 1920s and a small Frank Lloyd Wright house in Great Neck.

An outstanding structure of national importance is the Saddle Rock Grist Mill, built around 1700 of massive hand-hewn timbers and restored by the County of

Onderdonk House, Manhasset

Grist Mill, Roslyn

Nassau to its operating condition of the early 1800s. The mill is one of the few operating tidal mills left in the United States.

Of major concern for preservation is the Onderdonk House in Manhasset, one of the few remaining Long Island buildings listed in the Historic American Buildings Survey of the late 1930s. This house, with a full two-story front portico, is one of the island's finest Greek Revival homes. Its interior has undergone considerable change and its use as a community meeting house does not guarantee a completely secure future.

Roslyn Area

Tucked in a small valley at the head of Hempstead Harbor, the Village of Roslyn has survived modernization, keeping many pre-1850 buildings intact. The village's four 18th-century structures include the Joseph Starkins House and the Roslyn Grist Mill on old Northern Boulevard.

The Grist Mill, now with a restaurant on its first floor, is one of the few remaining on Long Island and a massive effort is needed to restore it to its original state and condition. John Robinson received a grant from the town to erect the grist mill in 1698. Henry Onderdonk, a leading patriot, was its owner in 1790 when George Washington visited there. In 1916, the Hicks family transferred it as a museum to a private board of trustees. Restoration replaced the wooden siding with clapboards of imititation concrete, but the handhewn frame and flooring remain.

The village's most distinctive period, the first half and particularly the second

Roslyn Stores

Valentine House, Roslyn

quarter of the 19th century, is represented by more than 40 houses on Main Street and adjacent streets. In contrast to Northern Boulevard, Main Street is predominantly residential. The Roslyn Landmark Society, formed in 1960, persuaded the village board to acknowledge the historic area officially and to set up a Historic Area Board, but the district was not included in the village zoning law. The town and county have also officially recognized Main Street as an historic area. County plans to widen it have been shelved but an alternate route must be found.

The village has helped to preserve the Valentine and Starkins Houses, and a private organization has resold and restored other historic structures. Several vacant structures are deteriorating, and continued efforts are needed to educate owners on the possibilities and economic advantages of good restoration.

Another structure worth mentioning is Cedar Mere, in Roslyn Harbor, formerly the home of William C. Bryant. Overlooking Hempstead Harbor, the grounds were designed by Frederick L. Olmstead and the boathouse was probably designed by Calvert Vaux, both noted for their superb accomplishments in designing Central Park, Prospect Park and many others.

Starkins House, Roslyn

Cedar Mere, Roslyn Harbor

Oyster Bay

① SAGAMORE HILL
△1 OLD BETHPAGE AREA
△2 SEA CLIFF AREA

TOWN OF OYSTER BAY

The Town of Oyster Bay, near the Suffolk County border, has 118 square miles of land and 360,000 persons in its 18 villages and unincorporated areas. Population growth has drastically changed its small communities, but a great deal of open space remains.

Its architectural heritage is hard to discern, although many fine pre-1860 farmsteads remain along the winding roads and high residential zoning apparently protects them at present. Among the great estate mansions is Sagamore Hill, Theodore Roosevelt's home, a good example of the rambling, shingled late-Victorian homes which once dotted the area.

Sagamore Hill, Cove Neck

Schenck House, Old Bethpage

Old Bethpage Village Restoration Area

Nassau County is constructing the Old Bethpage Village Restoration off Round Swamp Road on the Nassau-Suffolk County line. Part of the County Historical Museum's program, the restoration is designed to save a significant number of architecturally and historically important structures from destruction on their original sites and at the same time to recreate the environment and activities of a pre-Civil War rural village on Long Island.

The village will have more than 20 restored buildings when it opens, after five years of preparation, and eventually more than 50 buildings. The Powell Farmhouse, the only building originally on this 220-acre site, is a rambling house with additions and changes made from the mid-1700s to mid-1800s. The Schenck and the Peter Cooper Houses, from Manhasset and Hempstead, both have outswept front eaves revealing the Dutch influence on local architecture. The Hewlett House from Woodbury is a fine example of a Georgian gambrel roof farmstead. The influence of Federal and Greek Revival styling on simple country homes is evident in the Conklin and Kirby Houses, small village homes from the Village of the Branch and Hempstead, and in an interesting Methodist circuit church from Manetto Hills.

The village will preserve several special-use structures of the type which has disappeared most rapidly: the Noon Inn from East Meadow, the Layton and Luyster Stores from East Norwich, a Hicksville blacksmith shop, the Prime Thimble Factory from Huntington, and the brick Potter House from Great Neck special attention is given to such accessory buildings, as barns, outhouses, carriage sheds and small shops; the carpentry shop and carriage building the Williams Farm complex are prime examples.

Sea Cliff Area

In 1871 a large Methodist campgrounds was established in what is now the Village of Sea Cliff and by 1883 the area

Layton Store, Old Bethpage

Williams Carpenter Shop, Old Bethpage

Victorian House, Sea Cliff

had enough year-round residents to incorporate as a village. The section bounded today by Prospect, Carpenter, Littleworth Lane and Boulevard Avenue is a delightful reminder of life in the gay 90s.

On a sharp hillside overlooking the harbor, this mixed commercial and residential area has many picturesque narrow lanes, twisting steep streets and small parks and play areas with towering trees. The more than 100 structures remaining from before 1900 show almost every late Victorian style, from fanciful iron-crested mansard roof homes jutting from steep hillsides to bracketed Carpenter Gothic houses adorned with fretwork.

Most of the buildings are well kept and realty values are high. Until recently the community generally was apathetic about architectural value, and continued leadership is needed to improve deteriorating structures and to retain the area's distinctive Victorian atmosphere.

Gothic House, Sea Cliff

Babylon

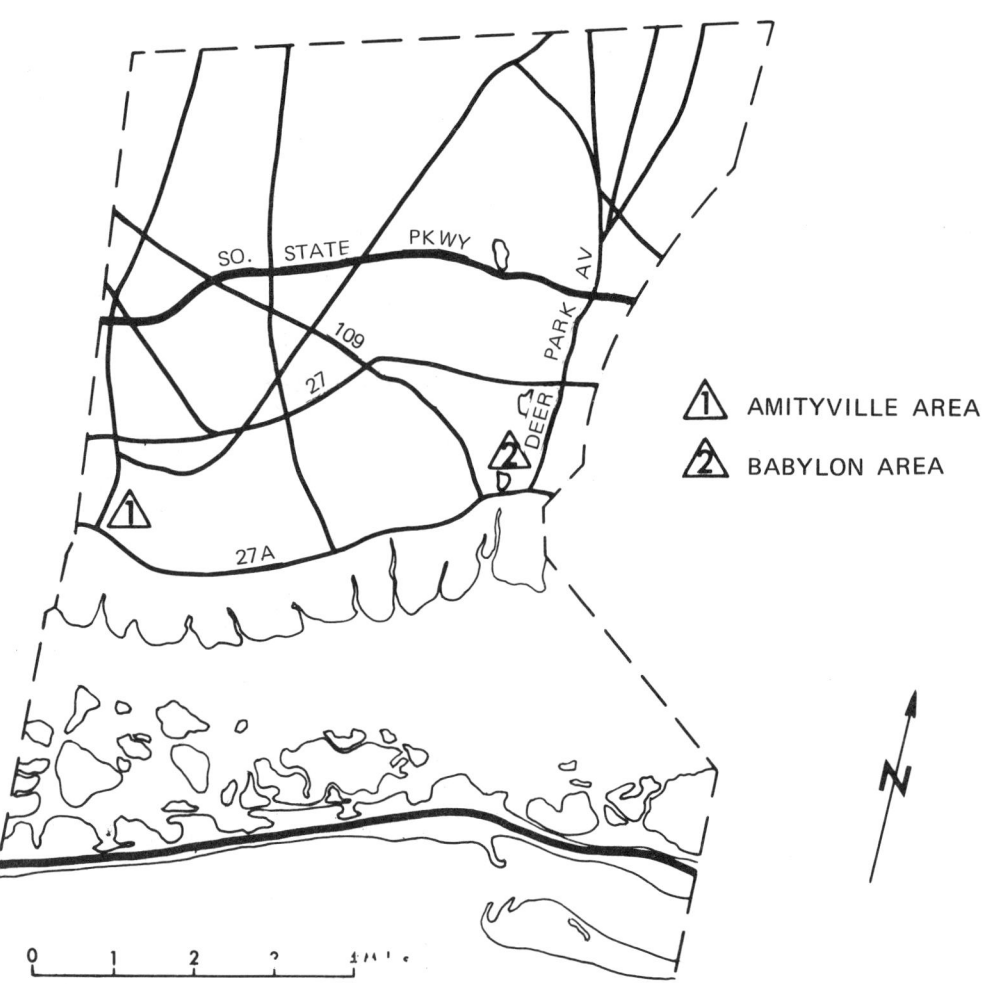

TOWN OF BABYLON

The Town of Babylon, in the southwestern corner of Suffolk County, has 192,000 residents, 71 square miles and three incorporated villages. Few older buildings of architectural distinction remain, so that preservation of several areas becomes even more urgent.

Amityville Area

One representative area, a long block on Broadway in Amityville, preserves the atmosphere of the early and mid-Victorian period, with some dozen structures from the 1840 to 1890 period. The tree-lined street has already been widened. Although it is principally residential, business zoning and business uses threaten it.

Broadway House, Amityville

Victorian House, Amityville

Deer Park Avenue
Store, Babylon

1826 House,
Babylon

Babylon Area

The center of Babylon has become a concentrated business and commercial area, but an area of interest is Deer Park Avenue from Route 27A north to Ellen Street. Many structures from the mid to late 19th century were either intended for commercial space on the ground floor and housing above or have been converted to business. Of particular interest are the mansard roof buildings on Deer Park Avenue at its intersections with Grove Place and Route 27A, and a dozen other structures, including the historic Conklin House, scattered along the avenue. Many buildings are deteriorating and a general restoration and repair campaign could provide a street of considerable architectural interest.

Conklin House, Babylon

Brookhaven

△1 BELLPORT AREA
△2 CENTER AND EAST MORICHES AREA
△3 MOUNT SINAI – MILLER PLACE AREA
△4 PORT JEFFERSON AREA
△5 SETAUKET, EAST SETAUKET, STONYBROOK, OLDFIELD AREA

Bellport Academy

TOWN OF BROOKHAVEN

Brookhaven is the largest town in Suffolk County, with 326 square miles and some 200,000 residents and seven villages. The great influx of population since 1960 has brought serious problems in almost every facet of community life. Much of the town's great rural charm are the many historic homes of good architectural quality, but efforts to preserve this charm are hampered. The size of the town, stretching from Long Island Sound to the Great South Bay, makes townwide efforts difficult yet often the influences affecting preservation are beyond the control of the villages.

The formation of a Town Historic Trust in 1968 is encouraging; it could provide decisive leadership in achieving an unequalled aesthetic inheritance.

Bellport Area

Among the interesting buildings and hamlets lining South Country Road is Bellport, a small community between the road and Great South Bay. One section which has escaped modernization contains some two dozen structures from the late

Gazebo, Bellport

Havens Homestead, Center Moriches

Leuthardt Barn, East Moriches

Academy Free Library, Miller Place

1700s to late 1800s, most from the early and middle 1800s. Tall trees add to the charming background, and the residents' interest is evident in the excellent condition of most structures.

Center Moriches-East Moriches Area

Route 27A, despite many changes of name, can never be mistaken. It is lined with structures of yesterday, generally undisturbed since the turn of the century, and is a fine scenic roadway.

The section from Lake Avenue in Center Moriches to Woodlawn Avenue in East Moriches has about two dozen buildings depicting the range of country architectural styles from throughout the 1800s.

Mount Sinai-Miller Place Area

Shore Road, Bayview Avenue and North Country Road in Mount Sinai, and Pipe Stove Hollow Road and North Country Road in Miller Place, are lined with Long Island farmhouses of the 1700s and early 1800s, some 40 houses, churches and stores dating from 1710 to the mid-19th century.

The Miller Place Academy is a fine example of Federal symmetry. Another superior building is the Millard House, built in 1710 by William Miller, a grandson of

37

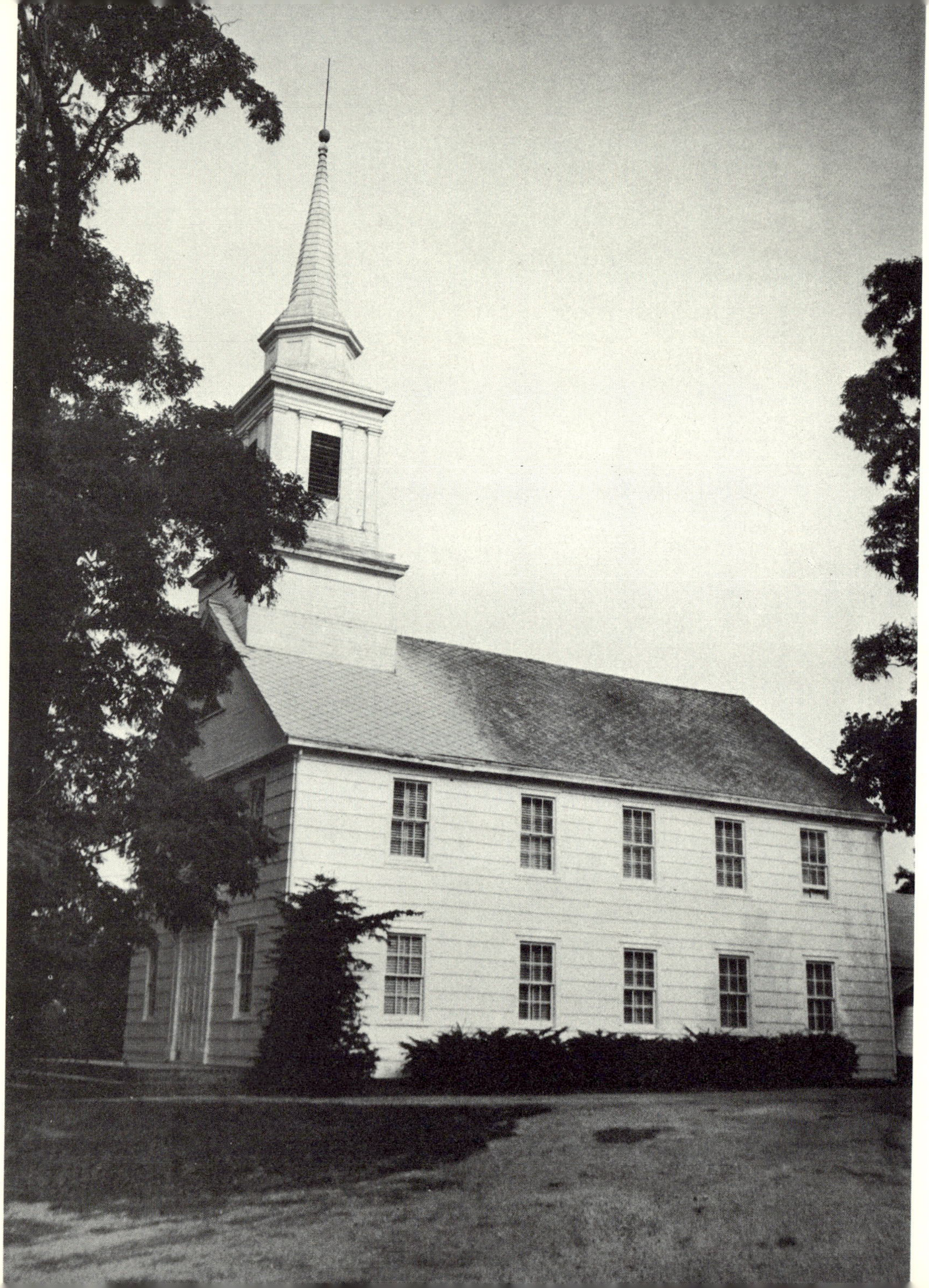

Millard House, Door

the founder of Miller Place, with additions in 1750 and 1816. This one-story partial saltbox house is three rooms wide, the Georgian detail of the front entrance adding an unusual architectural flourish.

Some properties are in only fair condition, and the houses' worth has been overshadowed by the nearby Setauket-Stony Brook complex. External threats result from the new State University, population increase and road improvement. The university may be expected to stimulate development and any major highway program affects large numbers of older homes because they are usually near roadways. A Connecticut-Long Island bridge, accelerating population growth and bringing major changes in land use and density patterns, would make older homes still more vulnerable.

Port Jefferson Area

Between the Stony Brook and the Miller Place areas is Port Jefferson, once the largest shipbuilding village on Long Island. Now a commercial community, its central street still reflects the mid-1800s seaport activities.

The architecture is noted for bead and reel molding. Many structures are in mar-

Tuthill and Young Office, Port Jefferson

E. Main St. Port Jefferson

Congregational Church, Mount Sinai

39

Thompson House, Setauket

ginal condition and the pressures of growth and business use constitute a grave threat. Much greater community and individual efforts are needed if these buildings are to be preserved.

Setauket, East Setauket, Stony Brook, Old Field Area

The area north of the State University campus at Stony Brook, including East Setauket and the entire peninsula to Long Island Sound, is a museum of Long Island and early American architecture. In this predominantly residential area, well over 100 structures depict Colonial and Federal styles from 1700 to the mid-1800s. Many churches and historic sites are open to the public, including the Thompson House, Sherwood-Jayne House and the Suffolk Museum.

This area provides a textbook on 18th century building techniques. The New England saltbox is illustrated by the Thompson House, operated by the Society for the Preservation of Long Island Antiquities. The Isaac Smith House is the standard two-and-a-half-story version popular through the Greek Revival period.

The houses are well maintained, their general condition is good and public interest is high. The location here of the headquarters of the Society for the Preservation of Long Island Antiquities, the strongest private historic preservation

Sherwood-Jayne House, East Setauket

Mount House, Stony Brook

organization, provides additional protection. Old Field has two-acre zoning and the remaining portions are in the Town of Brookhaven, which has been responsive to residents' desires. Still, massive problems result from growth around the new State University, the nearby Levitt housing development and continuing population influx.

Ward Melville, a strong supporter of architectural preservation, has purchased and restored many important buildings, including the Mount and the Brewster Houses. Through his wide ownership, he also exercises control through restrictive covenants in deeds which require his approval for exterior changes.

East Hampton

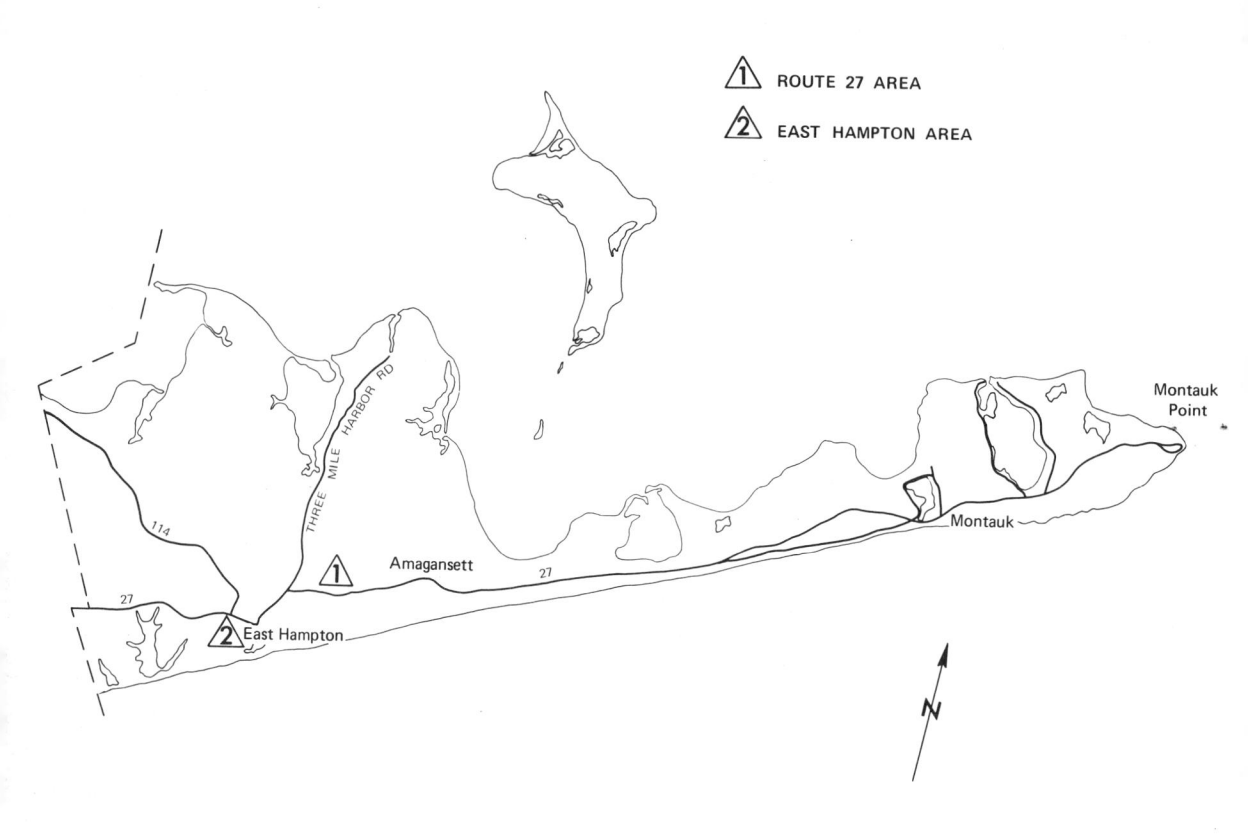

△1 ROUTE 27 AREA
△2 EAST HAMPTON AREA

Montauk Point
Montauk
Amagansett
27
East Hampton
114
THREE MILE HARBOR RD
27

0 1 2 3 4 Miles

N

42

TOWN OF EAST HAMPTON

East Hampton, on the south fork, is the farthest east town in Suffolk County. It has more than 12,000 persons and 72 square miles of land.

Route 27 Area

State Route 27 (Montauk Highway) provides a continuous scenic atmosphere on the south fork of Long Island through the Towns of East Hampton and Southampton. Beginning at Canoe Place, paralleling Shinnecock Bay, and heading eastward through Southampton to Montauk Point, the route has many fine early 18th to mid-19th century structures, especially from the Federal period.

Long stretches through Shinnecock Hills and east of East Hampton and Amagansett have relatively few landmarks, but the richness in East Hampton and Bridgehampton amply compensates. No other stretch of roadway in the state has so many fine landmarks open to the public and the surviving windmills at Bridgehampton, Watermill and East Hampton make this stretch unique in the United States. The John Payne House and Windmill in East Hampton are well cared for, and are of prime historical and architectural interest.

Hook Mill, East Hampton

East Hampton Historical Museum

Public interest makes most of the area secure, but one major landmark is threatened: Montauk Lighthouse, built in 1795 at the very end of the town. The U.S. Coast Guard will eventually abandon it and plans must be formulated now to acquire and preserve the lighthouse from the encroaching ocean. This is a major effort, but this is one of the most significant structures within the entire area and on the East Coast.

Elsewhere, commercial intrusions, generally on the outskirts of the villages, must be controlled to retain compatible environments for the remaining good structures.

A limited-access Route 27, which already stretches from Canoe Place to Southampton, will eventually relieve economic pressure on the older roadway out to Amagansett.

John Payne House, East Hampton

Montauk Lighthouse

45

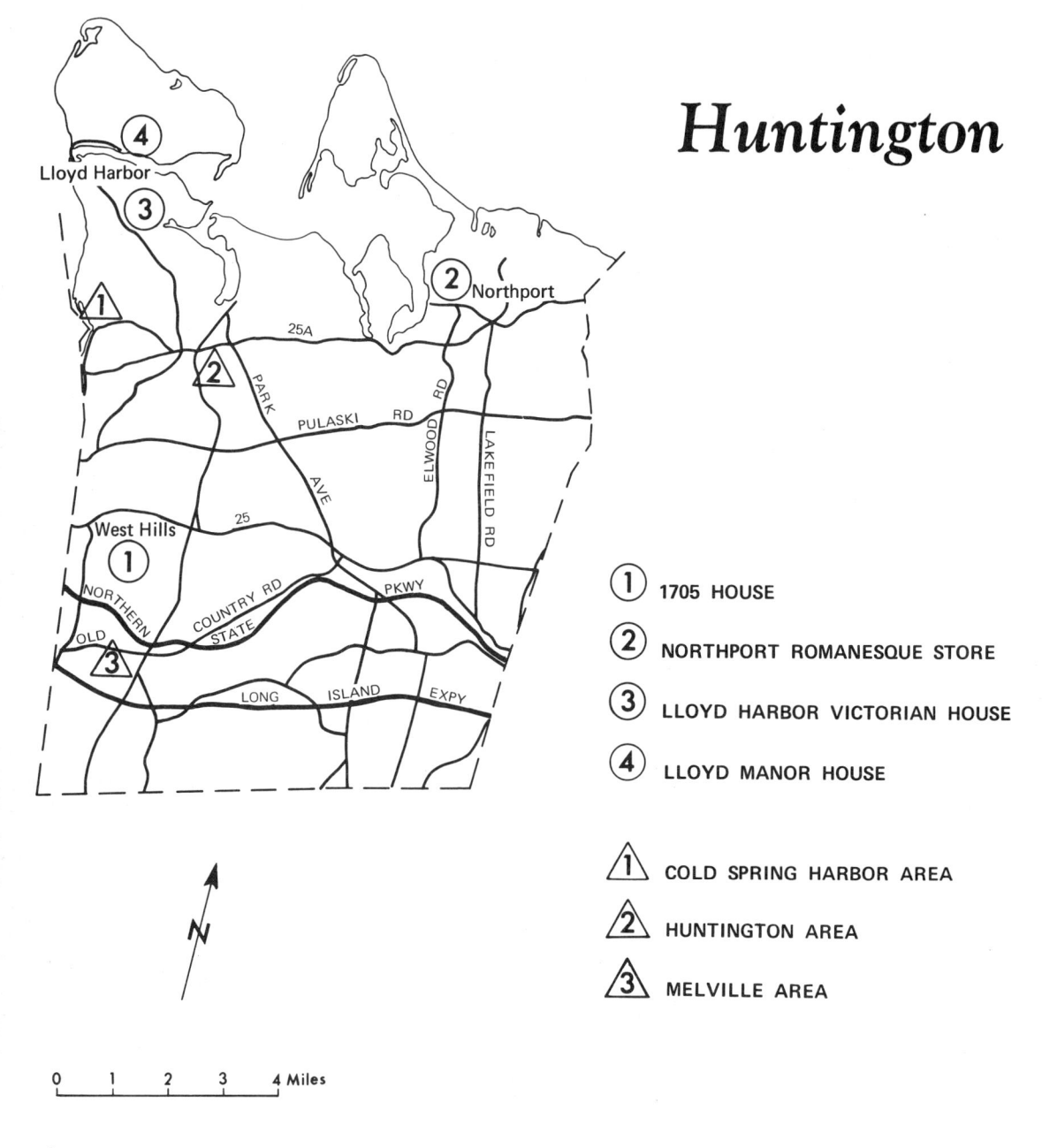

Huntington

① 1705 HOUSE
② NORTHPORT ROMANESQUE STORE
③ LLOYD HARBOR VICTORIAN HOUSE
④ LLOYD MANOR HOUSE

△1 COLD SPRING HARBOR AREA
△2 HUNTINGTON AREA
△3 MELVILLE AREA

Store, Northport

1705 House, West Hills

Victorian House, Lloyd Harbor

TOWN OF HUNTINGTON

Huntington, in northwestern Suffolk, has four incorporated areas and 182,000 residents within its 94 square miles. Several areas have considerable numbers of fine structures: West Hills, Northport and Lloyd Harbor all have important architectural resources.

Scattered structures of special architectural interest include the Lloyd Manor

Lloyd Manor House, Lloyd Harbor

House on Caumsett, Marshall Field's estate. The Long Island State Park Commission has acquired this early colonial saltbox, which should be preserved in developing the park.

Recognizing the problems for many privately owned homes, the town has established a Historic Sites Commission to determine needs and to develop a preservation plan before suburban growth engulfs the remaining heritage.

Cold Spring Harbor Area

This former whaling seaport retains considerable maritime flavor, with many structures from the late 1700s to mid-1800s on Harbor Road, Main Street, Shore Road and adjacent side streets. Most are residences, although many on Main Street have been put to commercial uses without too great a sacrifice of exterior details.

The condition of structures is generally very good, but development of Caumsett

Residence, Cold Spring Harbor

Residence and Store, Cold Spring Harbor

State Park could be a major threat to the entire area if careful planning and design are not provided. The extension of Bethpage State Parkway, to run along Harbor and Shore Roads, could destroy many beautiful buildings. The Long Island State Park Commission is planning this road carefully to retain the area's unique atmosphere, and it is hoped will safeguard architectural and historic landmarks.

Main Street Store, Cold Spring Harbor

Octagonal House, Huntington

Main Street Residence, Cold Spring Harbor

Jarvis-Fleet House, Huntington

Huntington Area

Despite tremendous growth and modernization in Huntington, a sizeable area at the east end of Main Street retains the character of almost two centuries ago. Here are several dozen notable examples of Federal architecture as well as other buildings from the early 1700s through the mid-1800s. Heckscher Park and Museum and the village green provide rural green pockets while nearby westward blocks contain interesting houses from the middle to late 19th century, including an octagonal house.

Located adjacent to the Thomas Powell house which was recently acquired by the Huntington Historical Society, the Jarvis Fleet House at 424 Park Avenue is in need of strong support for restoration. This major two-and-a-half-story, shingled, gambrel roof house may date back to 1679, when David Phillips acquired the property. Captain William Jarvis bought this property in 1688 and made substantial additions, including possibly the handsome pine paneling in the dining room. The building underwent other additions and was owned by the family of Samuel Fleet, prominent educator, publisher and newspaper owner.

Melville Area

Old Country Road, west of Sweet Hollow Road and east to Whitman Road, is another oasis of yesteryear. Although the area has no single distinctive building, a church and half a dozen residences from the early to mid-1800s relieve the architectural monotony of surrounding suburbia. These typical Long Island farmhouses, in their undisturbed setting, provide an air of unusual tranquility.

Islip

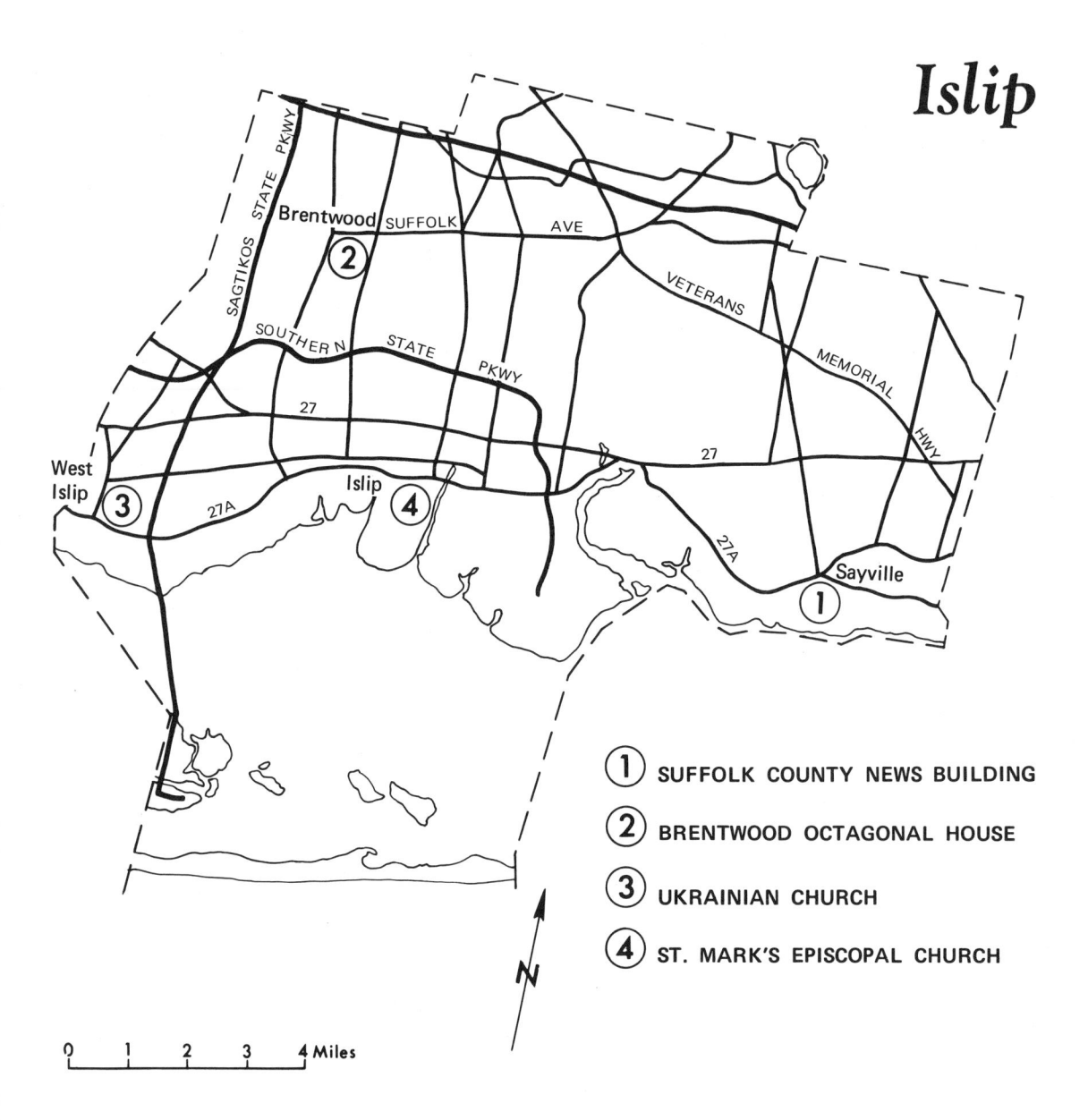

① SUFFOLK COUNTY NEWS BUILDING
② BRENTWOOD OCTAGONAL HOUSE
③ UKRAINIAN CHURCH
④ ST. MARK'S EPISCOPAL CHURCH

Suffolk County News Building, Sayville

Rector's House, Brentwood

TOWN OF ISLIP

Three villages and 258,000 residents are in the 136 square miles of the Town of Islip. Suburban growth has left only scattered structures of quality architectural feeling.

Many, such as the Suffolk County News Building, with Classic Revival one-story columns, have been converted to business use and have an uncertain future. Future developments along Route 27A must be watched carefully to protect some interesting structures along the highway.

The town contains an unusual number of architectural oddities. The several octagonal buildings in Brentwood, remnants of a mid-1800 utopian community; a Ukrainian church with near-Eastern influence in West Islip; and St. Mark's Episcopal Church in Islip, an eclectic early-1900s structure with a strong flavor of the historic Norwegian stave church — all are structures of great interest and value.

Ukrainian Church, West Islip

St. Mark's Episcopal Church, Islip

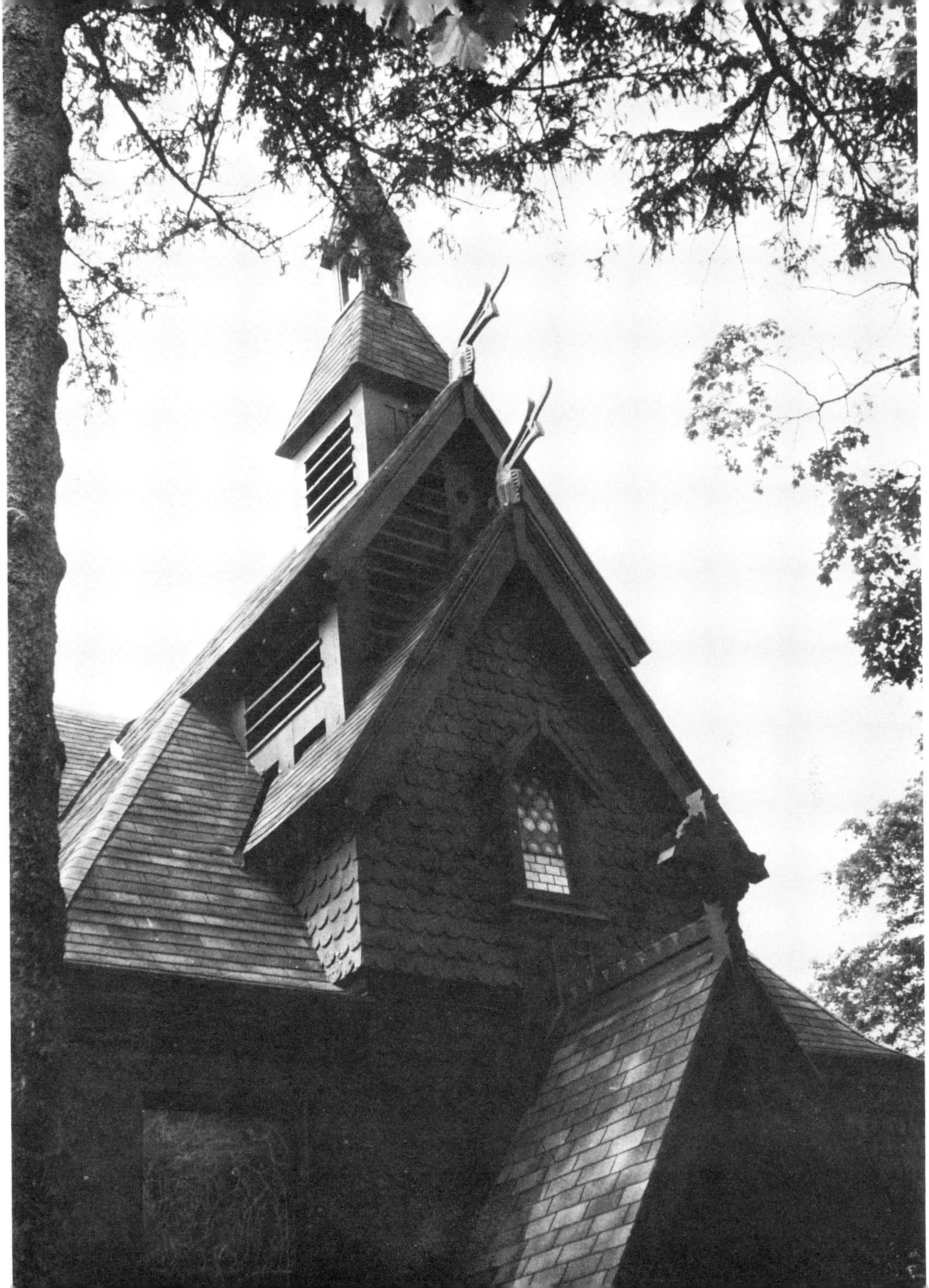

Riverhead

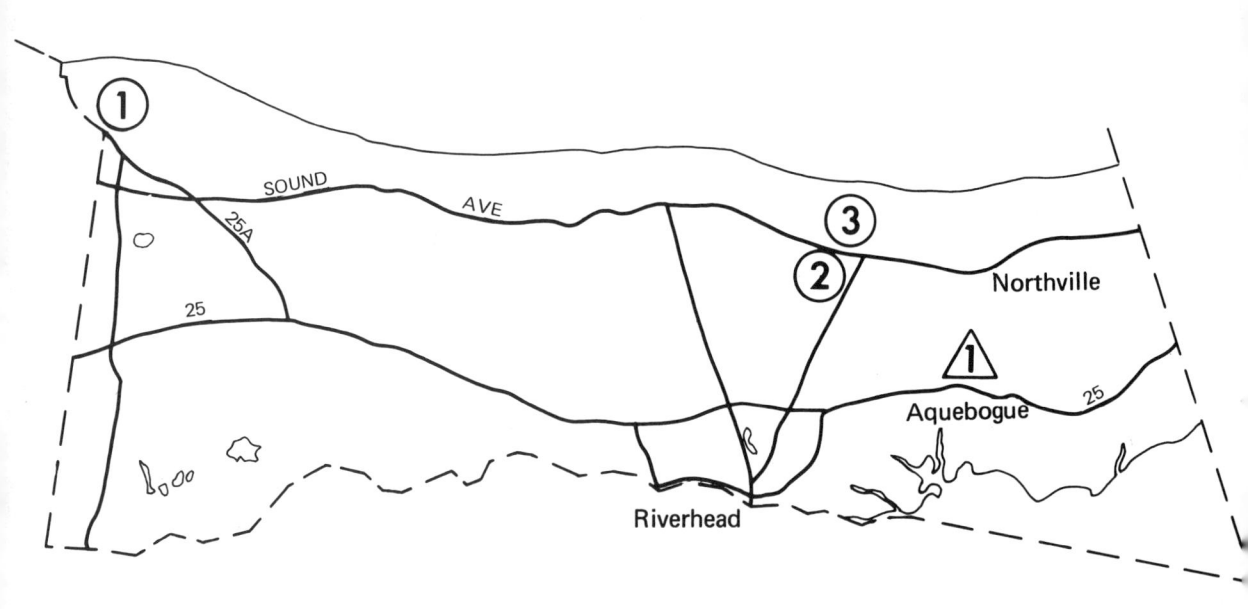

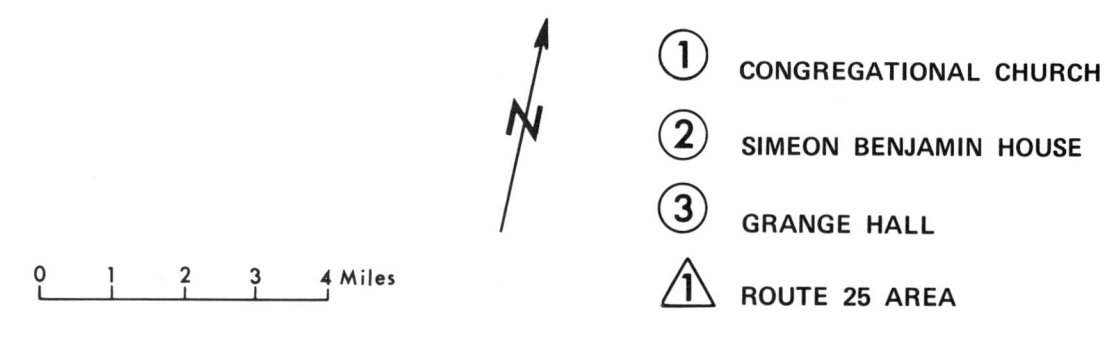

① CONGREGATIONAL CHURCH
② SIMEON BENJAMIN HOUSE
③ GRANGE HALL
△1 ROUTE 25 AREA

Church,
Wading River

TOWN OF RIVERHEAD

Riverhead, one of the two towns on Suffolk County's north fork, has a population of about 18,000 and an area of 68 square miles.

Much of the Town of Riverhead is still open farmland, and in its small complexes of farm buildings are some 18th and 19th century buildings. Several are in Wading River, including a fine Congregational church with an interior balcony, and others

Simeon Benjamin House, Northville

are scattered along the North Road and Sound Avenue.

Among those with an uncertain future is the Simeon Benjamin House in Northville, a gambrel roof, center-chimney house built in the 1820s.

Route 25 Area (Town of Riverhead only)

Among the first Long Island areas to be settled was its slender north fork. This area had strong ties with New England, and many 18th century buildings convey a New England atmosphere. As Route 25 leaves Riverhead, the first well-kept early 19th century home, surrounded by colorful gardens, sets a tone that continues through the rest of Riverhead and through Southold.

In Aquebogue, both sides of Route 25 are lined with colonial homes from the early 1700s through the mid-1800s — the familiar saltbox, the typical Long Island half-house and the long rambling one-story houses of the mid-1700s, with massive center chimneys. The structures continue through Laurel, some apparently not cherished.

Grange Hall, Northville

Route 25 House, Laurel

59

Shelter Island

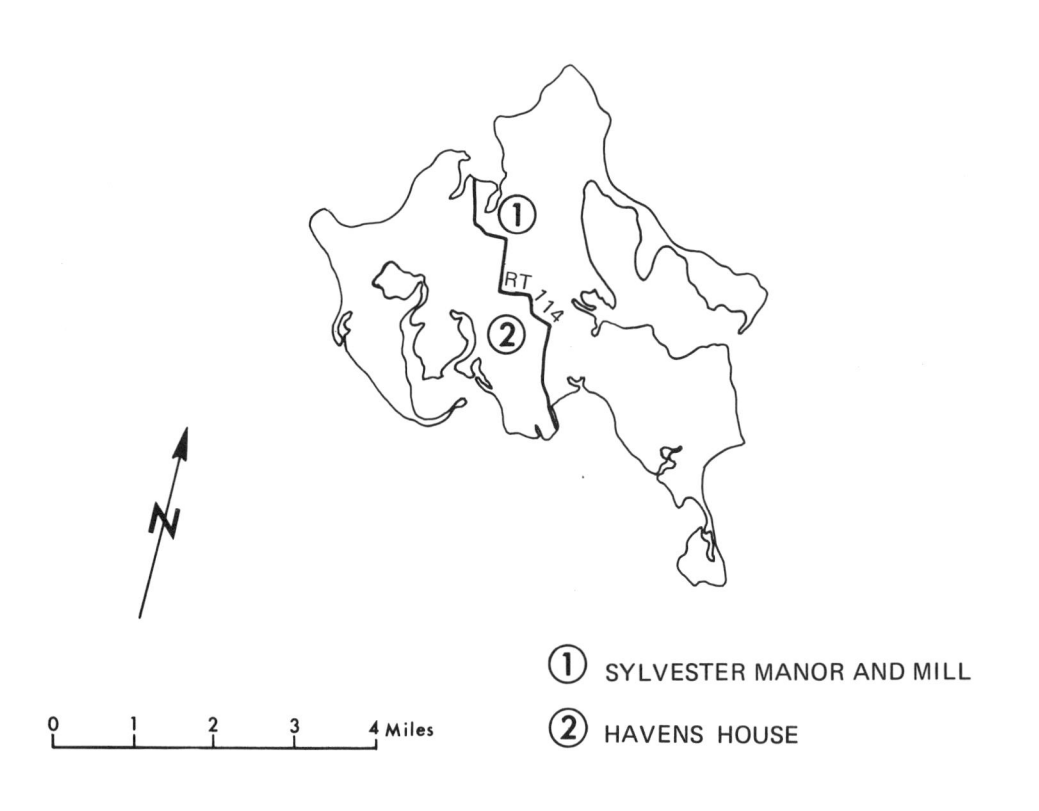

① SYLVESTER MANOR AND MILL
② HAVENS HOUSE

Sylvester Windmill, Shelter Island

TOWN OF SHELTER ISLAND

The only town not connected with the mainland is Shelter Island, 11 square miles with a population of 1,600. Isolated between the two forks of eastern Suffolk County and accessible only by ferry and boat, Shelter Island retains a pastoral quality that is not likely to change the character of a previous generation's quiet summer retreat with unpretentious homes.

The scattered early distinctive buildings include the Sylvester Manor windmill, one of the county's last remaining such structures. Sylvester Manor House and the Havens House also remain from the early 18th century, along with some delightful examples of late Victorian rambling summer homes with interesting fretwork.

61

Sylvester Manor, Shelter Island

*Havens House,
Shelter Island*

Smithtown

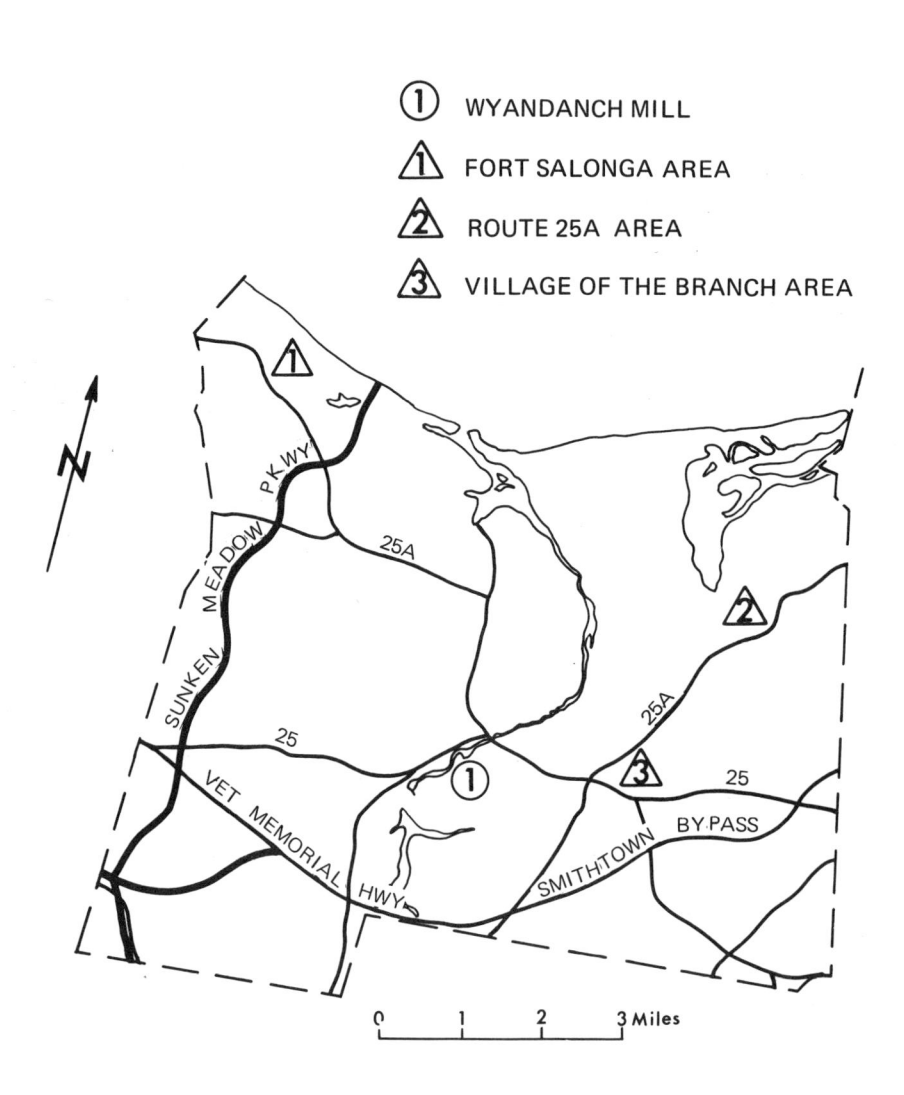

① WYANDANCH MILL
△1 FORT SALONGA AREA
△2 ROUTE 25A AREA
△3 VILLAGE OF THE BRANCH AREA

Lamb House, Fort Salonga

TOWN OF SMITHTOWN

Smithtown, facing Long Island Sound, has an area of 54 square miles and a population which has doubled since 1960, to 100,000. As in Huntington to the west, suburban residential growth and commercial activity along its major roads are rapidly changing the town. Most of its scattered older structures are well cared for; the major threat is to the few remaining along key roadways.

The Wyandanch Club combines natural and historic interest and its structures include a mill built in 1795. The Long Island State Park Commission, which leases this property to a hunting club, should safeguard these worthwhile structures.

Fort Salonga Area

On Route 25A between Sunken Meadow and Bread and Cheese Hollow Road is another small area of undisturbed Federal and early 19th century architecture. Approximately nine houses from the

65

St. James Railroad Station, Route 25A Area

late 1700s to the mid-1800s, in good condition, provide a residential area of considerable atmosphere.

Route 25A Area

Route 25A from Smithtown northeast to the Brookhaven town line provides a continuous view of Federal structures. Along the road are three 18th century houses, a hotel, more than a dozen early 19th century houses and half a dozen from the Victorian era. Route 25A, basically residential with some commercial uses, ties in with the Village of the Branch to the south and with Stony Brook-Setauket to the north.

Community response has blocked, at least temporarily, any widening of 25A, and a commission has been proposed to suggest ways of preserving the road's special character. Major points are Head of the Harbor, with a dozen fine structures, and a small complex at the Mills Pond Road intersection, dominated by an imposing columned Greek Revival mansion.

Also of interest is the St. James Railroad Station, near Route 25A just outside Head of the Harbor. Built in 1873 and now restored to its original condition, this is the earliest building of the Long Island Rail Road which still remains.

Mills Pond House, Head of the Harbor

Village of the Branch Area

This tiny incorporated area along heavily developed Middle Country Road (Route 25) is an unspoiled oasis of late 17th century and early 18th century architecture. Throughout Nassau and the Towns of Huntington and Smithtown, the route is a garish, haphazard and usually ugly commercial slash across the countryside. But for 4,000 feet eastward from the intersection with Route 25A, it is lined with stately white colonial homes of the late Federal period.

The Smithtown Presbyterian Church, although outside the village, is an outstanding landmark. Along Route 25 near Route 25A are the Brush House, the Presbyterian Church Rectory and Walt Whitman's Schoolhouse, all from the early 1800s. Farther, on the north side, fine homes dating from 1726 to 1845 illustrate various Federal styles in a rural setting. The historic Hallock Tavern, with its narrow windows and charming proportions; the Caleb Smith House, a public historic site of the Smithtown Historical Society; and four early 19th century structures on Judges Lane remain undisturbed.

Although the Village of the Branch has the only architectural district law in Long Island, widening of Route 25 would

Presbyterian Church, Smithtown

Brush House, Village of the Branch

destroy or impair almost every structure if land is taken from the north side. The State Department of Transportation has stopped action on this project and several alternates are under study.

Severe economic pressure makes it essential to preserve exterior features of buildings already converted to business and professional uses. It does not appear now that any structures must be moved, although the Conklin House was moved two years ago to the Old Bethpage Village restoration. The small village needs continued support in its efforts to preserve its architectural heritage.

Hallock Tavern, Smithtown

Caleb Smith House, Smithtown

Southampton

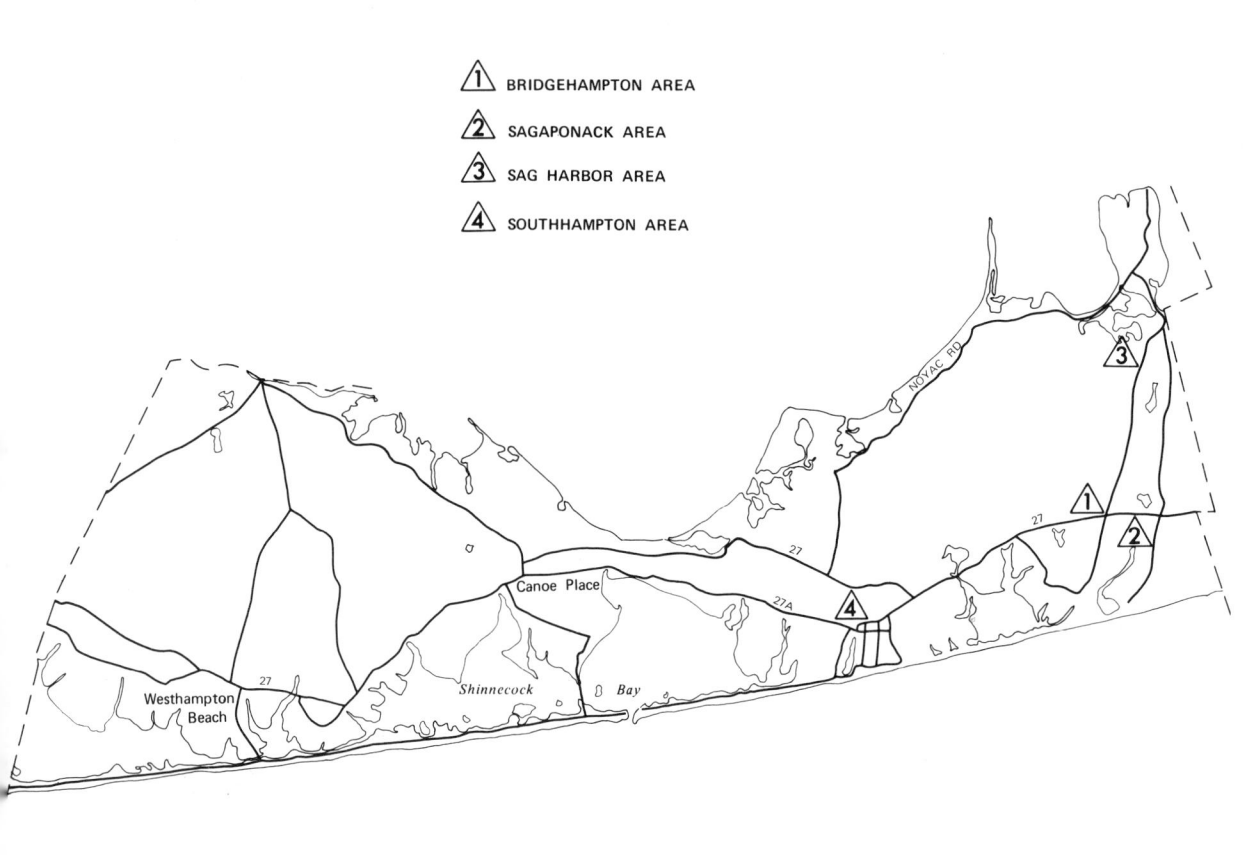

△1 BRIDGEHAMPTON AREA
△2 SAGAPONACK AREA
△3 SAG HARBOR AREA
△4 SOUTHHAMPTON AREA

Windmill, Bridgehampton

TOWN OF SOUTHAMPTON

The Town of Southampton, between Peconic Bay and the Atlantic Ocean, has an area of 171 square miles, more than 34,000 people and five villages. It and East Hampton form the south fork of Long Island's tip.

Routes 27 and 27A (discussed under East Hampton) are a key to the future of many architecturally fine structures in Southampton. The town also has a surprising amount of other architectural wealth, much of it undiscovered. Increasing realty values and the exclusiveness of many communities protect most of the buildings, but despite the residents' reluctance to attract more population, information on these structures should be recorded and disseminated so that interested people can help in their preservation.

Church, Bridgehampton

Bridgehampton Area

In the center of Bridgehampton, Route 27 is lined with stunning buildings; Ocean Avenue, School Street and Hildreth Lane continue this atmosphere. The side streets have particularly noteworthy Greek Revival structures among some 25 buildings from the late 1700s and the early 1800s.

Hampton House, facing onto Montauk Highway, is one of the best Greek Revival

Hampton House, Bridgehampton

structures in the state, with two-story Ionic columns across its front center. The local pride typified by its recent repainting holds out a bright future for the area.

Sagaponack Area

The several miles of Sagaponack's Main Street from Route 27 south to Bridge Lane are a stretch of almost unchanged Federal homes, interspersed with farm fields. Early saltbox homes illustrate the pre-Revolutionary period. This area deserves more recognition as a street of notable early 18th century architecture.

Salt Box, Sagaponack

Sag Harbor Area

Sag Harbor ranks among the best communities in the United States for Federal and Greek Revival architecture. On its short, narrow blocks, more than 100 homes exhibit the best design of the mid-1700s to the mid-1800s. The shopping center has many contemporary building. Several fires have destroyed waterfront landmarks

Custom House, Sag Harbor

Jared Wade House, Sag Harbor

and the adjacent business section, but a tremendous collection of residences still makes this village outstanding.

These homes are throughout most of the village, but mostly on Main, Madison, Suffolk, Jefferson, Garden Bay and Division Streets, Jermain Avenue and many small connecting blocks.

Their quality matches their quantity. Many were constructed by craftsmen with a fine sense of harmony, proportion and line, in the total structure and in the smallest detail of trim. The classical doorways are probably unmatched in variety of style, the Van Scoy and Jared Wade Houses being good examples. Cornice development is exceptional, including hand-wrought rope moldings of the Greek Revival period, as in the Abraham Vail house.

Small cottages like the Wade and Prime Houses are common, but a few conspicuous Greek Revival mansions provide contrast — such as the Whalers' Museum with Corinthian columns, the massive Whalers' Church by Minard Lafever, and many sizeable residences. There are even some fine mid-century mansard and gingerbread trimmed houses, all evidence of the material benefits in this once prosperous whaling community.

Old Whalers' Church, Sag Harbor

Whaling Museum, Detail

Whaling Museum, Sag Harbor

Residence, Sag Harbor

Halsey House, Southampton

Southampton Area

The entire center of Southampton has many colonial structures, with an atmosphere of federal America on Jobs Lane, Meeting House Lane, South Main Street and adjacent streets. The rerouting of 27A has reduced traffic on Jobs Lane, a commercial section of fine shops, many in early to mid-19th century buildings. On Main Street below Jobs Lane are gracious Federal homes and the Halsey House, a well restored 17th century structure. The Southampton Colonial Society has restored a complex on Meeting House Lane, centered around the Captain Albert Rogers home, a fine Greek Revival structure.

The structures are in very good condition, property values are extremely high and landmark structures are highly desired as residences. Commercial pressures on the village must be controlled, however, to assure their future.

Southold

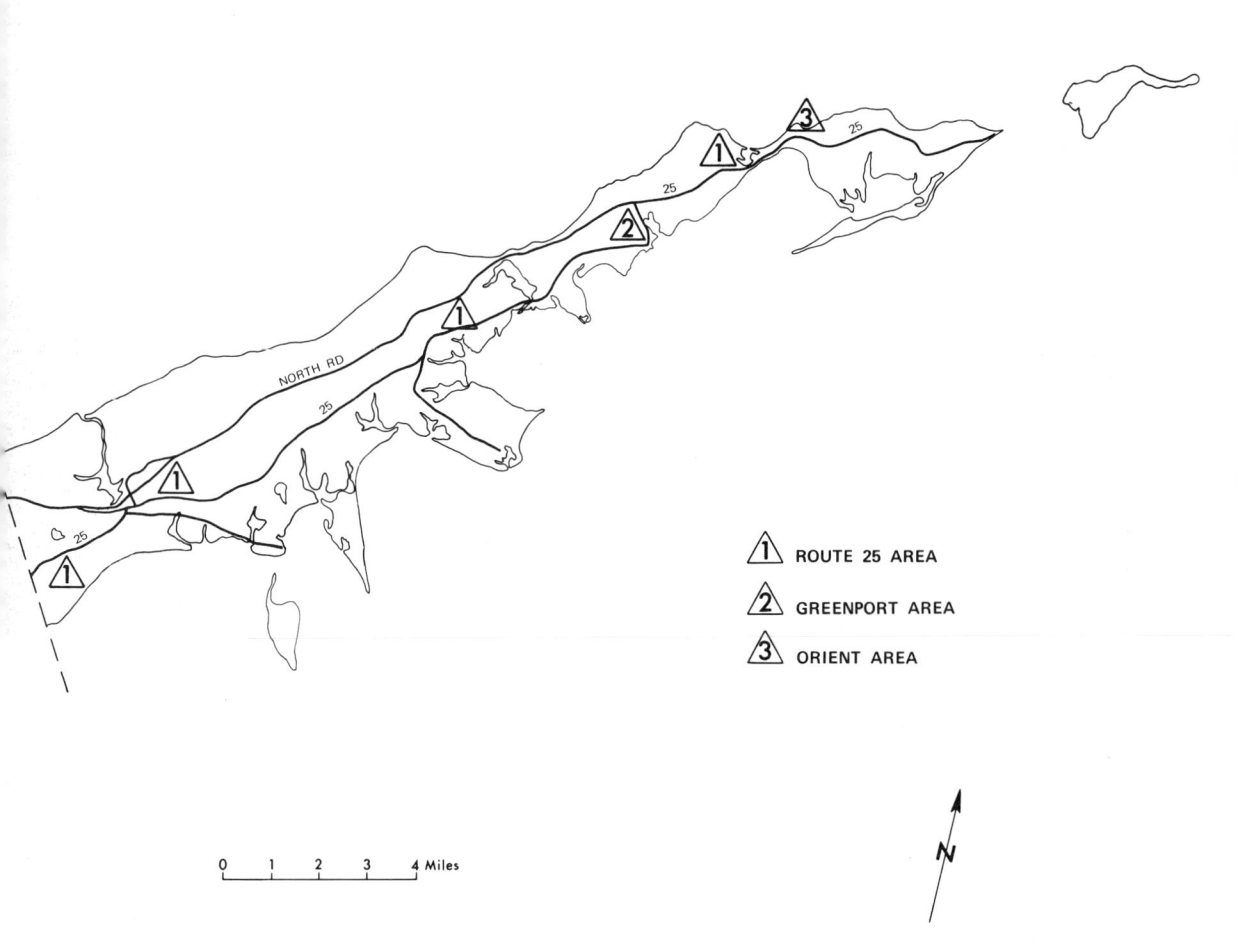

△1 ROUTE 25 AREA
△2 GREENPORT AREA
△3 ORIENT AREA

0 1 2 3 4 Miles

N

78

Residence, Route 25A, Laurel

TOWN OF SOUTHOLD

The easternmost town on the north fork of Suffolk County is Southold, with more than 16,000 residents in 54 square miles. This town, covering most of the north fork, is the earliest settled portion of the island and was under strong English influence from the earliest colonial times.

This influence is very evident in the Route 25 Area, which runs to the very tip of the fork and is lined with architecturally important buildings. However, the poor condition of many is a dangerous omen.

With many significant buildings throughout the town, its inheritance is perhaps the richest on the island. The buildings are widely scattered along the two waterfronts and appear in clusters and great frequency along Route 25.

Octagonal House, Mattituck

Old House, Cutchogue

Route 25 (Town of Southold)

In Mattituck, a large octagonal building compensates for a small business section which interrupts the distinctive rural mood of the road. A major landmark at Cutchogue is the medieval-like Old House, built in the 1640's. This atmosphere continues to the point of the fork through Southold, East Marion and Orient, the latter two heavily endowed with exceptional 18th and early 19th century buildings.

The Schaefer House at East Marion, known historically as the Harmon Tuthill House, was in the Schaefer family until the 1950s but is now vacant. Amon Tabor III, a local craftsman noted for his doorways and woodwork, built this typical one-and-a-half story half-house. Its doorway is a masterful example of Greek Revival style, with two Ionic columns and a transom with blue glass.

Orient Point Inn housed British troops in the American Revolution and remained a famous hotel until 1967, but today is vacant and threatened by vandalism. This is probably the largest pre-Civil War building on Long Island, its main section built in the late 1700s, with a massive four-story front facade with eight-over-twelve-pane windows.

Orient Point Inn

*Schaefer House
Door Detail*

*Schaefer House,
East Marion*

Main Street Stores, Greenport

Main Street Residences, Greenport

Townsend Manor Inn, Greenport

Along this entire route are relatively few modern intrusions, and house after house exhibits characteristics of the early 18th to the early 19th century. A number of public historic sites make a vacationist's delight. The majority of structures are well cared for, but a disturbing number need repair; recognition as a scenic route could arrest commercial excesses. The area has active historical societies, but their resources are inadequate for the area's pressing preservation needs.

Greenport Area

The least recognized area of architectural and historical merit on Long Island is the center of Greenport, overshadowed by extraordinary colonial architecture elsewhere. Main Street from Route 25 south to the harbor, Carpenter Street paralleling it, and adjacent streets have almost 100 structures from the first half of the 19th century.

The area is predominantly residential, but the lower end of Main Street is completely commercial. Along upper Main and Carpenter Streets is a wonderful variety of building styles from 1820 to 1860, when the village was a maritime center. These include fine late Federal homes and such distinctive Greek Revival and early

Victorian buildings as the Townsend Manor Inn complex. On Main Street leading to the harbor are commercial facades little changed since the Civil War, while near the still active waterfront is one of the few operating blacksmith shops on Long Island.

The community is little aware of its special resource. Some fine buildings have deteriorated and more than an average number are for sale. Community education would show how these architectural assets could bolster Greenport's weak economy by making it an interesting and exciting vacation resort. Numerous restaurants and an extensive waterfront are ideal ingredients. As an incorporated area, Greenport can control its own zoning and has some influence over its development.

Orient Area

Orient's Main Street from Route 25 to the waterfront is a small street bypassed by

Victorian House, Orient

modernization. This street and a few adjacent blocks have more than a dozen structures of architectural value, from the late 1700s to mid-1800s.

The Oysterponds Historical Society has preserved several structures but the condition of others varies and several are for sale.

Main Street Residence, Orient

Webb House, Orient

Part III

Programs for Preservation

COMPREHENSIVE PROGRAM

This survey identifies many areas and buildings of appreciable value, although by no means all distinctive structures. It does indicate the geographic breadth and historical depth of Long Island's architectural resources. Some landmarks are rimmed by a sea of split-level homes, others are intimately grouped in quaint village settings and still others are set amidst acres of greenery and splendid landscape. The range of use and condition is broad: from professionally preserved to privately violated, from private home to public site, from restaurant to office and from visual asset to decaying antique.

Within this overall context is cast the challenge of preserving Long Island's architectural heritage. Techniques for preservation must recognize the geographic scope and diversity of the island's landmarks; the numerous levels of jurisdictions; the wide range of uses; the constant pressure for new roads and schools; the diverse demands for public funds; the conservatism of lending organizations; the profit motive of builders; and our limited knowledge of landmark structures and of good preservation practices.

How can we safeguard the sense and mood of yesterday's existence for tomorrow? How can we assure our children and their children of experiencing the flow of history in everyday surroundings?

Responses must be varied and continuous. While no one all-encompassing solution can be championed, the major elements of a comprehensive program can be delineated for public and private review, discussion and ultimate action. Essential principles include:

Knowledge. The initial step in a preservation program is a complete survey of all notable buildings, including in-depth information on each building's location, detailed description, condition, use, history and present owner.

Awareness. The knowledge derived from such a survey must be disseminated to make the general public and various groups aware of the community's heritage. Landmark owners should be told about the significance of their structures, professional groups such as historians, architects and planners should evaluate the relative merits and suggested priorities, political leaders should be alerted to the implications of alternate courses of action, civic and business groups should recommend ways to blend such structures with new development. Finally, the public must be aware of their heritage in order to provide grassroots support for preservation.

Preservation plan. A preservation plan may have several variations. It is usually a list of landmarks based on the survey, with professional recommendations on priorities considering each landmark's relative merit and the threats to it. Then the local governing body or planning board evaluates priorities, suggests the roles of various private and public groups and proposes a tentative action program. After public hearings and private discussions with various concerned groups produce a consensus, the governing body and planning board can formally approve the plan, following public announcements of support by groups essential to the preservation program.

Public and private cooperation. The preservation program must have the cooperation of public and private sectors of the community. Government and banks can cooperate with owners in expediting repair and restoration. Architects and historians can provide technical assistance. Local governing bodies and planning boards can cooperate with civic and business groups in obtaining full community support. Public and private groups can work with banks to develop lending policies which aid preservation.

Helpful tools and programs, discussed in sections on the private and public sectors, should be evaluated carefully, to choose the methods most appropriate for the particular community.

PRIVATE SECTOR

The private owner, individual or corporate, at present bears the major burden of landmark preservation on Long Island, and a variety of economic problems make it difficult to maintain a landmark. Real estate taxes have risen tremendously and in many areas land has become more valuable than the building on it. Repairs and maintenance cost more for historic structures. Still, most owners derive a sense of personal satisfaction from preserving the landmarks they live or work in. Landmarks are also an intangible asset to the community; their continued use spans the gulf of history by keeping the old relevant to our dynamic society.

For this worthwhile task, a private owner generally needs technical advice and financial assistance. He can obtain technical advice through local historical societies and such public agencies as the Nassau County Historical Museum at Salisbury Park or the New York State Historic Trust in Albany. But, other than personal credit, a private owner has no sources of financial assistance. Even a fiscally responsible owner frequently finds that banks vary on granting mortgage loans for acquiring or restoring landmarks.

The commercial owner, however, may be able to maintain his landmark by converting it to a contemporary business activity without destroying its basic character. Restaurants are a frequent use — for example, the Milleridge Inn in Jericho, where an original colonial building is now part of a restaurant and tourist complex. Landmarks are also ideal for small office operations, such as real estate brokers, lawyers, architects and insurance agents. Many small businesses in Cold Spring Harbor show how with tasteful imagination an architectural landmark enhances business potential. In this way preservation serves an economic as well as a social and educational function.

Historic Societies

Efforts by historical organizations to extend knowledge and to provide technical assistance on the uses and preservation of landmarks can encourage private restoration, for residential or business uses. Useful information on the aesthetic and economic value of landmarks helps to dispel the owner apathy which deters preservation. An excellent example is the Roslyn Landmark Society in Nassau County, whose vigorous activities of the last six years have aided the restoration of many houses by private owners. Other small societies are active, such as the Oysterponds Historical Society at Orient, which maintains three structures.

The Society for the Preservation of Long Island Antiquities, with headquarters in Setauket, is the largest and best financed restoration group in Suffolk County. Its information collection, surveying and maintenance of six landmarks throughout the island have had considerable influence. By collecting information on the technical aspects of preservation and by properly surveying landmark structures, the society has developed a body of knowledge valuable to the professional and to the private owner.

Other historic societies must conduct public education programs, to make average citizens aware of their architectural heritage. This requires complete and accurate information on landmarks, obtained through research and field surveys.

Preservation Corporations

Long Island is an ideal location for preservation activity by a corporate organization. Since World War II some local restorations have preserved exteriors while renovating interiors for modern uses. Ward Melville has done this in the Stony Brook area, and a private group of investors in Roslyn has acquired properties and found owners who will follow this procedure. The necessary combination of imagination and money is rare, but this approach has succeeded in many communities throughout the country, such as Providence, Georgetown and Charlestown, and could provide a major inpetus on Long Island. Local citizens could establish a non-profit, public benefit or membership corporation with a revolving fund to acquire, restore and resell landmark properties with an initial capitalization of $100,000.

Gifts

Owners of architectural landmarks should seriously consider how to ensure their future. Gifts to municipalities or local organizations are an excellent way, the donor continuing occupancy rights until death. Or the donor can make a bequest, stipulating conditions for future use. Such a gift provides great personal satisfaction to the donor, and the social satisfaction of preserving an important piece of the community fabric so that future generations may understand a little of their heritage.

The tax advantages of a gift made during the donor's lifetime are generally known. The value of the gift may be deducted from the adjusted gross income up to 30 percent. Over that amount, the undeducted portion may be carried forward for as long as five years. The donor also saves on capital gains taxes he would incur in selling the property at a profit.

Lending Institutions.

It is generally difficult to get financial assistance for acquiring and restoring landmarks. Banks and loan associations are reluctant to provide maximum mortgages for older structures because the loan usually exceeds the appraised value of the structure. Unfortunately, appraised values rarely indicate the total economic value of a landmark property.

Some loan institutions are aware of this broader value. A landmark like Sagamore Hill has direct economic value because it attracts tourists who spend money and generate commercial activity. Indirectly, well preserved landmarks help to stimulate a cultural environment and make the community more attractive for residents, newcomers and new businesses. All lending institutions should consider such broad economic factors rather than the simple appraisal of land and building value. One technique would be for all the banks in a community to set up a pool to provide mortgage money to owners of landmark properties. Such an enlightened approach would allow the success of private efforts.

PUBLIC SECTOR

Acquisition

All three townships in Nassau County have restored and maintain landmarks, and several villages have assisted local historical societies in this work. Nassau County, through its Historical Museum, has the largest such program on Long Island and one of the most extensive in the country, owning three landmark structures and the Old Bethpage Village restoration. Besides preserving many landmarks, the village will provide an excellent practical laboratory on quality preservation techniques and will increase interest throughout the bi-county region.

There is also wide preservation interest in Suffolk County, on both the town and village levels. Several towns are taking the first tentative steps toward establishing historic and architectural preservation commissions and some, such as Huntington, contribute funds to maintain local landmarks. In both counties, it is hard to obtain village financial support but there is increasing awareness of the possibilities of local preservation legislation.

Structures acquired by local government can serve usefully as community centers, libraries, golden age centers, government offices or adult education quarters. The financial burden is considerable, but high acquisition costs and spiraling construction costs often make public participation an absolute necessity.

A wide variety of new state and federal programs can help to meet capital costs if local maintenance is provided. Federal programs include the Historic Preservation, Open-Space Land, Urban Beautification and Urban Renewal programs of the Department of Housing and Urban Development. The State Historic Trust provides state and federal funds for preservation work in New York State.

A main responsibility of the Historic Trust is implementing a program of state grants-in-aid to municipal historic site projects, under Section 1-0803 of the Conservation Law. Grants cover up to 50 percent of the cost of acquiring or developing a municipal historic site. The basic requirements are:

> The historic site must be owned by a unit of local government;
>
> Its local historic importance must be established;

The municipality must agree to maintain the site according to regulations established by the State Historic Trust;

Completed plans for using the site for historic site purposes must be submitted.

Although funding by Congress is not yet adequate, some federal grants are available for local projects under the National Historic Preservation Act of 1966, the State Historic Trust administering funds for projects within the state. Further information on either program is available from:

> State Historic Trust
> Office of Parks and Recreation
> State Campus
> Albany, New York 12226

Assistance is also available under the Historic Preservation Program in Title VII of the Housing Act of 1961 as amended, administered by the U.S. Department of Housing and Urban Development. Section 709 provides for matching grants to local public bodies of up to half the eligible costs of acquiring, restoring or improving historic or architectural sites. Grants are also available for less-than-fee acquisitions such as an easement or protective covenant, and for moving structures. Conditions are:

Grants may be made only to states or local public bodies;

Projects must be in an urban or urbanizing area;

Projects must be approved by a local planning agency;

Applicants must make provision for continuing maintenance;

Provisions must be made for continuing public control.

The Open Space Land Program makes grants of up to 50 percent to public bodies to acquire land for open space purposes. These purposes include using open space for preservation or display of landmark property, acquiring landmarks valued separately at less than $25,000 and located on underdeveloped land, or acquiring acreage surrounding a landmark if the land will be used for open space.

The Urban Beautification Program provides for grants of up to 50 percent of the cost of improving historic landmarks through paving, plantings, fencing, special lighting and other improvements. These projects must be part of a community's comprehensive beautification plan.

Additional information on these federal programs may be obtained from:

Assistant Regional Administrator
for Metropolitan Development
Department of Housing and Urban
Development
26 Federal Plaza
New York, New York 10013

Federal funds may be used in an urban renewal area to restore an historic or architecturally valuable structure acquired by the local urban renewal agency or to relocate a structure which will be restored and maintained within or outside the renewal area. The restoration and/or moving of such structures is computed as local noncash grant-in-aid and goes towards paying the non-federal share of the urban renewal project cost. Further information on this program may be obtained from:

Assistant Regional Administrator
for Renewal Assistance
Department of Housing and Urban
Development
26 Federal Plaza
New York, New York 10013

*Preservation, Historic District
and Aesthetic Zoning Legislation*

In addition to financial assistance, a number of legal measures can advance preservation. In particular, local government must be aware of how historic district laws and aesthetic zoning regulations can protect superior architectural and historic values. The Village of the Branch is the only community in the region which has an historic district law. Other communities such as Roslyn, Lloyd Harbor, Huntington and Brookhaven have designated areas, attempted to obtain legislation, or have commissions studying the problem. The villages of Bellport and Southampton have valuable aesthetic zoning requirements.

Broad preservation powers have been given to county, city, town and village governments under a 1968 amendment to the General Municipal Law, empowering them to protect sites or structures of special historic or aesthetic interest or value. Protection can take the form of regulations, special conditions or restrictions and may also include control of the use and appearance of neighboring private property within public view.

Cities and villages, as part of their zoning powers, can designate historic districts. The local legislative body may regulate and restrict certain areas as historic landmarks or as special historic sites, places and buildings.

Municipalities also have the power to enact zoning laws which can regulate the appearance of new buildings, in accordance with standards adopted to preserve the character of areas with historic or architectural landmarks. The regulations governing community appearance are usually administered by an architectural review board which determines whether a proposed building meets the standards under the zoning law.

Landmarks Preservation Commission

A landmark preservation commission is the appropriate administrative agency to carry out local preservation or historic district legislation. The commission should have three main duties: to survey all landmark structures within its jurisdiction and establish records and descriptions; to designate landmarks which should be preserved and to establish procedures to implement legislation, including notification of owners, public hearings and issuance of permits; and to establish review machinery to insure that designated landmarks are not altered or demolished.

Such a commission should also offer advisory services to owners, to aid them in preservation and to alleviate any hardships caused by designation. Other auxiliary functions can include accepting gifts of landmarks to the municipality, and the restoring and maintaining of landmarks owned by the municipality.

Even without legislation, a local government can establish a landmarks official or bureau which has no enforcement powers but can provide professional guidance to the area's citizens. The activities of a local landmarks official or bureau should have these objectives:

To advance community appreciation of its architectural resources and their preservation. A public education program can accomplish this through such efforts as tours, literature and photographs.

To help local government and private owners overcome technical deficiencies in restoration. The landmarks bureau must develop technical knowledge about restoring and maintaining landmarks through staff experts or consultants and offer this knowledge through an advisory service.

To meet the critical need for information on architectural landmarks so that local planners, historical societies, individuals, businessmen and state officials can act effectively to preserve them. This information must be accurate, detailed and available.

This report and studies undertaken by the State Historic Trust provide general information, but a detailed building-by-building architectural study will provide the necessary explicit, vital data.

Survey and Designation

A permanent authoritative record of all architectural historical landmarks on Long Island is needed, after a survey based on professionally recognized standards like those of the Historic American Building Survey.

Landmark surveys can be conducted at the town, county or regional level. Federal assistance for up to two-thirds of the cost and state grants covering half of the local share are available under the Comprehensive Planning Assistance Program. This program covers the cost of determining which structures are of architectural or historic value and the feasibility of restoring them, as well as other necessary information. Towns which are engaged in or are about to undertake master planning studies can undertake such surveys and the Nassau-Suffolk Regional Planning Board could undertake a survey for all of Long Island as part of its regional planning program.

When it has adequate information about valuable structures, a local government should designate them as official landmarks. This has been done in several communities, including Roslyn and Huntington. Designation has minimum effectiveness as a preservation technique, but it does give official notice of a structure's value and focuses public attention on it. Community knowledge of its architectural or historical heritage is a prerequisite for broad-based support of preservation.

Comprehensive Planning Program

Local comprehensive planning programs can help to reduce the threats to landmarks which arise from community growth and development. By identifying existing and future physical, social and economic changes, and evaluating their impact upon the community's land use, a comprehensive plan can pinpoint long-range forces that have a definite effect upon landmark preservation. A short-range benefit is in aiding the resolution of conflicts between development and preservation, through accurate information on land use, zoning and marketability. An active comprehensive planning program is necessary for proper preservation and for community development, and local planning agencies should include landmark preservation in their land use and public improvement plans.

Information on the Comprehensive Planning Assistance Program may be obtained from:

    New York State Office of
    Planning Services
    488 Broadway
    Albany, New York 12207

Zoning and Subdivision Controls

The zoning power of local governments is an important tool for landmark preservation. Zoning is a legal tool to insure the reasonable use of land, to stabilize property values and to conserve existing economic buildings, and these goals can reduce the threats to landmarks. Because zoning regulations can control mixed land use, prevent over-intensive development and reduce uncertainty regarding community growth, they make for fewer pressures on landmark's than in an unregulated situation.

Subdivision control, another method to insure the reasonable use of land, is directed at predominantly open land which is proposed for division into separate parcels for sale or lease. Frequently a subdivision proposal calls for the demolition of a landmark to provide a few additional lots. In reviewing the subdivider's preliminary proposal, a local planning board should evaluate the possibility of retaining the landmark as part of the development. A planning board can require such preservation for the community's welfare in the same manner as it can require parks and other public works in a new development.

CONCLUSION

This report has described the wealth of architectural landmarks all over Long Island. Because of the almost overwhelming threats to their existence, this heritage cannot be taken for granted. Only the cooperative work of residents, political leaders, landmark owners, historical societies, bankers and many others can accomplish landmark preservation.

The goal of protecting our past in order to make our future meaningful is worthwhile and necessary. The past cannot be destroyed in the name of the future without ultimate realization that this created future is sterile and alien. Our future society must be built on the solid foundations of the past, and one foundation is the physical manifestations of this past — our architectural and historic landmarks.

Appendix

ARCHITECTURAL LANDMARK EVALUATION AND INDEX

Methodology

From the initiation of this study, it was realized that limitations of time and resources allowed only an evaluative, not a comprehensive survey. Several thousand buildings could have been added to the ones listed, but these include almost all prominent structures and others which indicate types and areas. The emphasis is on pre-1860 buildings; contemporary buildings are ones designed by noted architects or significant historically.

The survey was conducted in several steps:

— *Research.* All previous surveys and many secondary sources such as histories and architectural publications provided a work list of possible buildings.

— *Local contact.* A questionnaire was distributed to all local historians, historical societies and local governments. Knowledgeable people in each township — historians, architects, builders, government officials — were interviewed to obtain their recommendations, and liaison was established with persons conducting local surveys and with the Historic American Building Survey and the Long Island chapter of the American Institute of Architects.

— *Field inspection.* After qualified observers checked each structure in the field, an index card was made for each structure giving its community, exact location, present owner, historical connection, date of erection and status of present and future use. More than three-fourths of the structures were photographed on 35mm black and white film, from which 4" x 5" prints were prepared. The index cards and photographs will form a permanent archives.

Evaluation criteria

The index of landmark structures which follows this section is a concise guide to significant buildings, by county and township. It lists commonly known names, street addresses or general location and landmark value.

— *Date.* Rather than using unsubstantiated dates, each structure has been assigned a date range based on known historic data or visual observation of its characteristics:

1700s	— all pre-1800 buildings
e 1800	— up to 1835
m 1800	— 1835 to 1875
L 1800	— 1875 to 1900
1900	— 1900 to date

— *Architectural value.* A value scale on the comparative architectural significance of each structure descends in importance from 1 to 3. The index is not comprehensive, but covers an estimated 40 percent of the landmarks on Long Island, particularly those in values number 1 and 2.

(1A) — *Present historic site or public use*

Structure owned, preserved and maintained by historical, government or other public organizations as a landmark.

Designation as National Historic Landmark and of architectural value.

(1) — *State and national significance*

Area: A publicly designated historic district.

An outstanding group of six or more related buildings illustrative of an architectural period and/or providing exceptional atmosphere of an earlier period.

Structure: A major structure within such an area.

Work of a major architect or builder.

Outstanding example of architectural style.

Outstanding example of early special use structure (industrial, etc.).

Of special architectural interest as a rare survivor, curiosity, special construction, or significant historical association.

(2) — *County and town significance*

Area: A group of related buildings preserving the atmosphere of an early period.

Structure: A major structure within such an area.

Outstanding example of architectural style within its county and town.

Outstanding example of special architectural interest or historical association and use.

(3) – *Local significance*

Structure: One of the best remaining examples of its architectural period, or of important local historical association.

Use. The present use of the structure is coded in the following ways:

PO – Private owner, either individual or special organization.

HS – Public historic site or used for public purposes.

V – Vacant.

B – Business or industrial.

Future status. Visual evidence, examination of public works plans and information from interviews provided the basis for identifying the future preservation status:

S – Secure against foreseeable threat.

No known destruction plans.
In protection historic district.

In properly zoned area, no economic or commercial pressures, good area.

ET – Eventual threat of destruction.

In deteriorating area, improperly zoned, economic and commercial pressure evident.

IT – Known destruction plans.

On site of pending public or private improvements.

Structure in poor condition.

99

LANDMARK INDEX
Nassau County

LOCATION	DATE	VALUE	USE	STATUS
HEMPSTEAD				
Garden City:				
Hilton Ave., Cathedral Ave., blocks adjacent to Garden City Hotel	L 1800	2	PO	S
NORTH HEMPSTEAD				
Roslyn:			PO	
Main St., Broadway, Bryant Ave., Old Northern Blvd.	L 1700 m 1800	1	B V	S ET
OYSTER BAY				
Old Bethpage:				
Old Bethpage Village restoration	L 1700 e 1800	1A	HS	S
Sea Cliff:				
Prospect Ave. to Littleworth Lane	L 1800	2	PO	S

Suffolk County

BABYLON				
Amityville:			PO	
Broadway, 50 through 119	e-L 1800	3	B	ET

Babylon:				
Deer Park Ave., 23 through 534	e 1800 1900s	3	PO B	ET
BROOKHAVEN				
Bellport:				
Academy Lane, Browns Lane	e-L 1800	3	PO B	S
Center-East Moriches:				
Montauk Highway (27A)	m-L 1800	3	HS PO B	ET
Mount Sinai-Miller Place:				
North Country Road	1700s e 1800	2	HS PO B	ET
Port Jefferson:				
Village core adjacent to Main St.	e-L 1800	2	PO B V	ET
Setauket, East Setauket, Stony Brook, Old Field:				
Areas north of 25A and Gully Road to Sound	1700s m 1800	1	HS PO B	ET
EAST HAMPTON-SOUTHAMPTON:				
Route 27 from Southampton to Amagansett	1700s e 1800	1	PO B HS	S ET

HUNTINGTON

Cold Spring Harbor:

Main St. between Shore Road and Goose Hill and radiating blocks, particularly to north	L 1700 L 1800	3	PO B HS	ET

Huntington:

Park Ave. around village green, particularly 25A	m 1700 m 1800	2	PO B HS	S

Melville:

Area near intersection of Old Country Road and Sweet Hollow Road	L 1700 m 1800	3	PO HS	S

RIVERHEAD AND SOUTHOLD

Route 25 from Aquebogue to Orient Point	e 1700 m 1800	1	PO B V HS	ET

SOUTHAMPTON

Bridgehampton:

Route 27, Ocean Ave. Hildreth and nearby	1700s e 1800	2	PO B HS	ET

Sagaponack:

Main St.	1700s e 1800	1	PO	S

102

Sag Harbor:				
Main St., Garden St., Union	1700s		PO	
St. and nearby blocks	m 1800	1	B	S
			HS	
Southampton:				
Route 27, Main St., Jobs Lane	1700s		PO	S
	e 1800	1	B	ET
			HS	
SOUTHOLD				
Orient:	m 1700		PO	
Main St.	m 1800	1	HS	S
Greenport:				
Main St. and adjacent	e-m 1800	1	PO	
blocks			B	ET
			V	
SMITHTOWN				
Route 25A, Smithtown to	1700s		PO	
Brookhaven line	m 1800	1	B	ET
			HS	
Fort Salonga:				
Route 25A between Sunken	1700s			
Meadow Road and Bread and	m 1800	3	PO	S
Cheese Hollow Road				
Village of the Branch:				
Route 25, Judges Lane	L 1700		PO	
	e 1800	1	B	IT

STRUCTURES

Nassau County

LOCATION	DATE	VALUE	USE	STATUS
HEMPSTEAD				
East Rockaway:				
Davison Mill, Woods Ave. and Denton	e 1800	1A	HS	S
Freeport:				
Old Oyster Wharf, South Main St.,	L 1800	3	B	ET
Raynor House, Mill Rd.	1700s	3	PO	ET
Garden City:				
St. Mary's Nursery School, 5th St.	L 1800	3	HS	S
Endo Chemical Co., Stewart Ave.	1900	1	B	S
Breed House, 113 Hilton Ave.	L 1800	3	PO	S
Residence, 95 Ninth St.	L 1800	3	PO	S
Apostle House, 40 Hilton Ave.	L 1800	3	PO	S
Cathedral, Cathedral Ave.	L 1800	1	HS	S
Hotel, 7th St.	L 1800	1	B	ET
Hempstead:				
St. George's Church, Front St.	e 1800	1	HS	S
Catholic Rectory, Greenwich St.	e 1800	3	HS	S
Methodist Church, Front St.	e 1800	1	HS	S
Cooper-Mott House, Clinton St.	e 1800	1	V	IT*
St. George's Rectory, Front St.	1700s	1	HS	S
VandeWater, Peninsula Blvd.	e 1800	2	V	IT
Snedecker House, Hempstead Tpk.	m 1800	3	PO	ET
Hofstra University dormitories, Hempstead Tpk.	1900	3	HS	S

*moved to Old Bethpage village restoration

Presbyterian Church, Hempstead Tpk.	m 1800	1	HS	IT
Greek Orthodox Church, 110 Cathedral Ave.	1900	3	HS	S

Hewlett:
Hewlett House, 86 E. Rockaway Rd.	1700s	3	PO	IT

Lawrence:
Rock Hall, Broadway	1700s	1A	HS	S

Mineola:
Old Court House, Franklin Ave.	1900	2	HS	S

Wantagh:
Railroad Station, Wantagh Ave.	L 1800	1	HS	S
R. Jackson House, 1542 Wantagh Ave.	1700s	3	PO	ET
Jerusalem Meeting House, Wantagh Ave.	e 1800	1	HS	ET

West Hempstead:
Residence, Nassau Blvd. and Cornwell	m 1800	3	PO	S

NORTH HEMPSTEAD

Albertson:
Searing Methodist Church, Willets Road	1700s	2	HS	S

Great Neck Estates:
F.L. Wright House, 9a Myrtle Dr.	1900	1	PO	S

Herricks:
Onderdonk-Foster House, Shelter Rock Road	1700s	3	PO	S

Manhasset:				
Manhasset Valley School, 25A	e 1800	1A	HS	S
Onderdonk House, 25A	e 1800	1	HS	ET
Quaker Meeting House, 25A	e 1800	2	HS	S
Mitchill House, South Dr.	e 1800	1A	HS	S
Old Westbury:				
Titus House, 21 Rt. 25	1700s	3	PO	ET
Phipps House, Old Westbury Road	1900	1A	HS	S
Willis-Post, Bacon Road	1700s	2	PO	S
Port Washington:				
Dodge House, 58 Harbor Road	1700s	3	PO	S
Roslyn:				
W. Valentine House, E. Broadway	e 1800	1A	HS	S
J. Starkins House, Main St.	1700s	1A	HS	S
Gerry House, Main St.	e 1800	2	PO	S
Roslyn Grist Mill, Old Northern Blvd.	1700s	1	HS	ET
Cedar Mere, Bryant Ave.	L 1800	2	PO	ET
Sycamore Lodge, Bryant Ave.	m 1800	3	PO	S
Residence, 94 Main St.	e 1800	3	PO	S
Residence, 20 Main St.	e 1800	3	B	S
Clock Tower, Main St.	L 1800	1A	HS	S
Roslyn Estates:				
Knothole, C. Morley Park	1900s	1A	HS	S
Saddle Rock:				
Grist Mill, Grist Mill Lane	1700s	1A	HS	S

Sands Point:
    Sands House, 195 Sands Point Road   1700s   2   PO   S
    Guggenheim Estate, Middle Neck Road   1900   2   PO   ET

Westbury:
    Hicks House, Rt. 25   e 1800   3   PO   ET
    Church of Advent, Rt. 25   1900   3   HS   S

OYSTER BAY
  Cold Spring Harbor: PO
    Cold Spring Military Academy, 25A   1900   2   HS   S
    Episcopal Church, Rt. 25A   e 1800   1   HS   S

  Cove Neck:
    Sagamore Hill, Sagamore Hill Road   L 1800   1A   HS   S
    Grey Cottage, Cove Neck Road   1700s   3   PO   S

  Farmingdale:
    Thomas Powell House, 55 Merritt Road   1700s   3   PO   S

  Glen Cove:
    Underhill House, Cedar Swamp Road   1700s   3   PO   ET
    Matinecock Meeting House, Duck Pond
      Road   1700s   1   HS   S
    Woolworth House, Crescent Beach Road   1900   3   B   S
    J.P. Morgan Estate, East Island   1900   3   HS   S
    Robert Coles House, 7 The Place   m 1800   2   PO   S
    Valentine House, The Place and
      Dickson Lane   1700s   3   PO   S
    Community Newspapers Building,
      147 Glen St.   e 1800   3   B   S
    R. Coles House, 34 The Place   1700s   2   PO   S
    Doubleday House, Meadow Spring   L 1800   3   PO   S

Jericho:
S. Underhill House, Rt. 25	1700s	3	PO	ET
Townsend-Jackson, Old Jericho Tpk.	1700s	3	PO	S
Maine Maid, Old Jericho Tpk.	1700s	3	B	S
Friends Meeting House, Old Jericho Tpk.	1700s	1	HS	S

Lattingtown:
The Creek Club, Horse Hollow Road	1900	3	B	S
Killingworth, Factory Pond Road	1900	2	PO	IT

Mill Neck:
Robert Deans Jr. House, Frost Mill Road	1700s	3	PO	S
Dudley F. Underhill House, Horse Shoe Road	1900	2	PO	S

Old Bethpage:
Old Bethpage Village restoration, Round Swamp Road
Schenck House	1700s	1A	HS	S
Kirby House	e 1800	1A	HS	S
Layton Store	m 1800	1A	HS	S
Luyster Store	e 1800	1A	HS	S
Hewlett-Jackson House	1700s	1A	HS	S
Manetto Hills Church	m 1800	1A	HS	S
Williams House and barns	e 1800	1A	HS	S
Conklin House	1700s	1A	HS	S
Powell Farm House	1700s	1A	HS	S

Old Brookville:
A. Youngs House, Hegemans Lane	e 1800	3	PO	S
Peterson Barn, Cedar Swamp Road	1700s	3	B	IT

Oyster Bay:
   Octagonal House, Spring St. and

W. Main	m 1800	2	B	IT
Raynham Hall, W. Main St.	1700s	1A	HS	S
Wightman House, 196 South St.	1700s	1A	HS	S
Youngs House, E. Main St.	1700s	2	PO	S

Sea Cliff:

Residence, 192 Prospect Ave.	L 1800	3	PO	S
Residence, 199 Prospect Ave.	L 1800	2	PO	S
H. F. Gould, 291 Glen Ave.	L 1800	2	PO	S
Fischer House, 87 Summit Ave.	L 1800	3	PO	S
Wm. Hogarth House, 209 Carpenter	L 1800	2	PO	S
J. Haynes House, 285 Glen Ave.	L 1800	3	PO	S
J. Marcusson House, 378 Glen Ave.	L 1800	3	PO	S

Syosset:

A. Underhill Barns, Underhill Blvd.	1700s	2	PO	IT
Schenck House, Convent Road	1700s	3	PO	IT

Suffolk County
BABYLON
  Amityville:

397 Merrick Road	m 1800	3	PO	ET

  Babylon:

Residence, 17 N. Carlls Ave.	e 1800	3	PO	ET
Store, Main and Deer Park Ave.	L 1800	2	B	ET
Carll House, 73 N. Main St.	e 1800	2	B	ET
Odd Fellows Hall, Deer Park Ave.	m 1800	3	B	ET
Store, Deer Park Ave. and				
Grove Place	L 1800	3	B	ET
N. Conklin House, Deer Park Ave.	e 1800	2	PO	ET
1801 House, W. Main St.	e 1800	3	PO	ET

BROOKHAVEN

Bellport:
Gazebo, Academy Road	m 1800	2	PO	S
Academy, Academy Road	e 1800	2	PO	S
Residence, S. Country Road	m 1800	3	PO	S

Brookhaven:
South Haven Church, S. Country Road	e 1800	1A	HS	S
Residence, Beaver Dam Road	e 1800	3	PO	S

Centereach:
New Village Congregational Church, Rt. 25	e 1800	3	HS	ET

Center Moriches:
Havens House, Montauk Hwy.	1700s	1A	HS	S

Coram:
Davis House, Rt. 25	e 1800	3	PO	ET

East Moriches:
Osborn House, Main St.	1700s	3	PO	S
Leuthardt Barn, Main St.	L 1800	3	PO	S

Eastport:
L.I. Country Club, Old Country Road	L 1800	3	PO	S

East Setauket:
Roe Tavern, Old Post Road	1700s	3	PO	S
Sherwood-Jayne House, Old Post Road	1700s	1A	HS	S
Brewster House, 25A	1700s	1	HS	S

Mastic:
Wm. Floyd House, Mastic Road	1700s	3	HS	ET

Middle Island:				
Presbyterian Church, 25A	e 1800	3	HS	ET
Miller Place:				
Durrin-Jennings House, Pipestave Hollow Road	e 1800	3	PO	ET
Millard House, N. Country Road	1700s	2	PO	ET
Academy Free Library, N. Country Road	e 1800	1	HS	S
Post Office, N. Country Road	1900	3	B	ET
Holiday House, N. Country Road	L 1800	3	V	IT
Whaley House, N. Country Road	1700s	2	PO	S
Mount Sinai:				
Congregational Church, N. Country Road	e 1800	1	HS	ET
Madsen House, N. Country Road	e 1800	3	HS	ET
Gracey House, N. Country Road	1700s	3	PO	ET
Kopcienski House, N. Country Road	1700s	3	PO	ET
Old Field:				
Lighthouses, Old Field Point	e-m 1800	2	HS	S
Smithwell House, Quaker Path	m 1800	3	PO	S
Patchogue:				
Residence, Gerard St.	e 1800	3	PO	S
Octagonal House, Maple and Oak St.	m 1800	2	PO	IT
Methodist Church, Ocean and Church St.	L 1800	3	HS	S
Residence, South and West St.	L 1800	3	PO	ET
Lace Mills, Merrick Road	L 1800	2	B	ET
Port Jefferson:				
Tuthill and Young Office, E. Broadway	L 1800	3	B	S

1812 House, E. Main St.	e 1800	3	B	S
Store, 214 E. Main St.	m 1800	3	B	ET
Rocky Point:				
Trinity Evangelical Lutheran Church, 25A	1900	3	HS	S
Setauket:				
Caroline Church, Strongs Neck Road	1700s	1	HS	S
Presbyterian Church, Caroline Ave.	e 1800	1	HS	S
Thompson House, Bennets Road	1700s	1A	HS	S
Elzon House, Bennets Road	1700s	2	PO	S
Shoreham: (vicinity of)				
Tesla Laboratory, Tesla St.	1900	2	B	S
Elmer House, N. Country Road	1700s	3	PO	ET
South Manor:				
Brookfield Presbyterian Church, Moriches Road	e 1800	3	HS	S
Stony Brook:				
All Souls Church, Main St.	L 1800	3	HS	S
Mount House, 25A	1700s	1	HS	S
No. 52 Main St.	L 1800	3	PO	S
Octagonal Building, Wayalawi Lane	m 1800	2	PO	S
Wading River:				
Seldoon Farm, N. Country Road	1700s	3	B	S
Historical Society, N. Country Road	e 1800	1A	HS	S

EAST HAMPTON

East Hampton:				
John Payne House, James Lane	1700s	1A	HS	S

J. Payne Windmill, James Lane	1700s	1A	HS	S
Mulford House, James Lane	1700s	1A	HS	S
Clinton Academy, Rt. 27	1700s	1A	HS	S
Hook Mill, Rt. 27	e 1800	1A	HS	S

Montauk:
Lighthouse, tip of island	e 1800	1	HS	ET

HUNTINGTON

Centerport:
Vacant House, 25A and Centerport Road	1700s	3	B	IT

Cold Spring Harbor:
Residence, Rogues Path	1700s	3	PO	S
Tannery, Rogues Path	m 1800	2	B	ET

Eaton's Neck:
Lighthouse, Eaton's Neck	e 1800	3	HS	ET

Huntington:
Jarvis-Fleet House, Park Ave. and Woodhull Road	1700s	1A	HS	IT
Octagonal House, Prime Ave.	m 1800	2	PO	S
D.A.R. House, 6 Nassau Road	m 1800	3	HS	S
Conklin House, High and New York Ave.	1700s	1A	HS	S
Presbyterian Church, Main St.	1700s	1	HS	S
Walt Whitman House, Walt Whitman Road	e 1800	1A	HS	S
Ezra Prime House, Spring Road	1700s	3	PO	S

113

Lloyd Harbor:				
Lefferts Mill, Southdown Road	1700s	2	PO	ET
Lloyd Manor House 1, Lloyd Harbor Road	1700s	2	HS	ET
Lloyd Manor House 2, Lloyd Harbor Road	1700s	2	PO	ET
Thom. Brush House, School Lane	1700s	3	PO	ET
Northport:				
Bryant-Skidmore House, 529 Main St.	1700s	3	PO	S
Hart Office, Main St.	L 1800	3	B	S
West Hills:				
Peace and Plenty Inn, Chichester Road	1700s	1	PO	S
Ezra Carll House, Melville and Barkers Lane		3		
Oakley-Gregory House, Sweet Hollow Road	1700s	3	PO	S
ISLIP				
Bayshore:				
Business bldg, S. Country Road	L 1800	3	B	ET
Business bldg, S. Country Road	e 1800	3	B	IT
Pentaquit Methodist Church, S. Country Road	L 1800	3	HS	S
Sagtikos Manor, S. Country Road	1700s	1A	HS	S
Brentwood:				
Episcopal Church, Third Ave.	L 1800	3	HS	S
Episcopal Rector's Octagonal House, 1769 Brentwood Ave.	m 1800	1	HS	S
Octagonal House, Second St.	m 1800	1	PO	ET

Islip:
    St. Mark's Episcopal Church, S.
        Country Road | 1900 | 2 | HS | S

Oakdale:
    St. John's Epsicopal Church,
        S. Country Road | 1700s | 1 | HS | S
    Bourne Estate, S. Country Road | 1900 | 3 | HS | S
    Sportsman's Club, Rt. 27 | 1700s | 3 | HS | ET

Sayville:
    Edwards House, Edwards St. | 1700s | 1A | HS | S
    Suffolk County News Building,
        Candee Ave. | m 1800 | 2 | B | ET
    Sayville Congregational Church,
        Middle Road | L 1800 | 3 | HS | S

West Islip:
    West Islip Ukrainian Catholic Church,
        S. Country Road | m 1800 | 3 | HS | S

RIVERHEAD

Aquebogue:
    Old Steeple Church, Rt. 25 | m 1800 | 3 | HS | S

Laurel:
    Residence, Rt. 25 | 1700s | 3 | PO | ET
    Residence, Rt. 25 | e 1800 | 3 | PO | IT

Northville:
    Meeting House, Sound Ave. | e 1800 | 2 | HS | S
    Congregational Church, Sound Ave. | m 1800 | 3 | HS | S
    S. Benjamin House, Sound Ave. | e 1800 | 2 | PO, V | ET

Wading River:
    Congregational Church, Sound Road   e 1800   2   HS   S
    Miller Home, N. Wading River Road   e 1800   3   PO   S

SHELTER ISLAND

  Sylvester Manor and Mill, Alt. Rt. 114   1700s   1A   PO   S
                                                                                                    HS

SMITHTOWN
Commack:
    Methodist Church, Town Line Rd.   e 1800   3   HS   S

Fort Salonga:
    Lamb House, Sunken Meadow Road   1700s   3   PO   S

Hauppauge:
    Methodist Church, Town Line Road   e 1800   3   HS   S

Head of Harbor:
    Stanford White House, Moriches Road   L 1800   3   PO   S
    Lefferts House, Moriches Road   L 1800   2   PO   S
    Mills Pond House, Rt. 25A   e 1800   1   PO   S
    Deepwells, Rt. 25A   m 1800   3   PO   S
    Timothy House, Rt. 25A   e 1800   3   PO   S

Kings Park:
    Obadiah Smith House, St.
        Johnland Road   1700s   1A   HS   S

Nissequogue:
- Malone House, Moriches Road — 1700s — 2 — PO — S
- Dixon House, Smith Lane — 1700s — 3 — PO — S
- Schabert House, Moriches Road — L 1800 — 3 — PO — S

Saint James:
- Episcopal Church, Rt. 25A — m 1800 — 3 — HS — S
- Railroad Station, Lake Ave. — L 1800 — 2 — B — S
- General Store, Moriches Road — L 1800 — 3 — B — S

Smithtown:
- Millers House, New Mill Road — e 1800 — 3 — HS — IT
- Wyandanch Club, Residence and Mill, Jericho Tpk. — e 1800 — 2 — HS — IT
- L.I.R.R. Trestle, Jericho Tpk. — L 1800 — 3 — B — ET
- Caleb Smith House, Rt. 25A — e 1800 — 1A — HS — ET
- Presbyterian Church, Rt. 25 — e 1800 — 1 — HS — ET
- Arthur House, Main St. — 1700s — 3 — HS — ET
- Methodist Church, Landing Ave. — e 1800 — 3 — HS — S
- Grist Mill, New Mill Road — e 1800 — 3 — HS — IT

Village of Branch:
- Thomas Brush House, Rt. 25 — m 1800 — 3 — PO — IT
- Turrell House, Rt. 25 — 1700s — 2 — PO — ET

SOUTHAMPTON

Bridgehampton:
- Sayrelands, Rt. 27 — 1700s — 1A — HS — S
- W. Corwith House, Rt. 27 — e 1800 — 1A — HS — S
- Presbyterian Church, Rt. 27 — e 1800 — 1 — HS — S
- Bulls Head Tavern, Rt. 27 — e 1800 — 2 — B — ET

Hampton House, Rt. 27	e 1800	1	PO	ET
Windmill, Hildreth Lane	e 1800	1A	HS	S
Quogue:				
Chapel, Main St.	m 1800	1A	HS	S
Schoolhouse, Main St.	1700s	1A	HS	S
Sagaponack:				
Residence, Main St.	1700s	2	PO	S
Sag Harbor:				
Custom House, Garden St.	1700s	1A	HS	S
Howell House, Main and Bayview	L 1800	3	PO	ET
Whalers' Church, Union St.	m 1800	1	HS	S
Whaling Museum, Main & Garden	e 1800	1A	HS	S
Municipal Bldg. Main St.	m 1800	3	HS	S
Van Scoy House, Main St.	e 1800	2	PO	S
Methodist Church, Division St.	m 1800	3	HS	S
Jared Wade House, Union & Madison St.	1700s	2	PO	S
French House, Main St.	m 1800	3	PO	S
Prime House, Madison St.	1700s	3	PO	S
A. Vail House, Madison St.	e 1800	3	PO	S
Hand House, Main St.	m 1800	3	PO	S
Southampton:				
Commercial Building, Windmill Lane and North Sea Ave.	e 1800	2	B	ET
Stores, 67 & 69 Jobs Lane	e 1800	2	B	ET
Halsey Home, S. Main St.	1700s	1A	HS	S
St. Andrews Church, Dune Road	L 1800	3	HS	S

Pelletreau Silver Shop, Main St.	1700s	3	HS	S
Capt. A. Rogers Home, Meeting House Lane	m 1800	1A	HS	S
Watermill:				
Windmill, Rt. 27	e 1800	1A	HS	S

SOUTHOLD

Cutchogue:				
W. Wickham House, Rt. 25	1700s	1A	HS	S
Old House, Rt. 25	1700s	1A	HS	S
Joshua Wells House, New Suffolk Lane	1700s	2	PO	S
East Marion:				
Schaefer House, Rt. 25	e 1800	2	PO, V	IT
Schneider House, Rt. 25	e 1800	2	PO	S
Residence, Rt. 25	m 1800	3	PO	S
Residence, Rt. 25	1700s	3	PO	S
Fishers Island:				
R. Neutra House	1900	1	PO	S
Greenport:				
Floyd House and Barn, Stirling locale, Rt. 25	m-L 1800	2	PO	ET
Townsend Manor Inn, Main St.	e 1800	2	B	S
Townsend Manor Inn Annex, Main St.	m 1800	1	B	S
Residence, 636 Main St.	m 1800	3	PO	S
Residence, 640 Main St.	m 1800	3	PO, V	S

Residence, 546 Main St.	e 1800	2	PO, V	IT
Commercial strip, Main St.	e-m 1800	3	B	ET
Mattituck:				
Octagonal Building, Rt. 25	m 1800	2	B	ET
Orient:				
Apartment House, Rt. 25	m 1800	3	B	ET
Residence, Main St.	e 1800	2	PO	ET
Methodist Church, Main St.	m 1800	3	HS	S
Webb House, Main St.	1700s	1	PO, HS	S
Residence, Main St.	m 1800	3	PO	S
Oysterponds Historical Society, Main St.	m 1800	1A	HS	S
Orient Point:				
Peakens Inn, Rt. 25	1700s	2	PO	S
Orient Point Inn, Rt. 25	e 1800	2	PO, V	IT
Southold:				
First Presbyterian Church, Rt. 25	e 1800	2	HS	S
American Legion Post, Rt. 25	L 1800	3	HS	S
Horton's Point Lighthouse	e 1800	3	HS	S
Ezra Hommedieu Home, Rt. 25	1700s	3	PO	S
Thomas Moore House, Rt. 25	1700s	3	PO	S

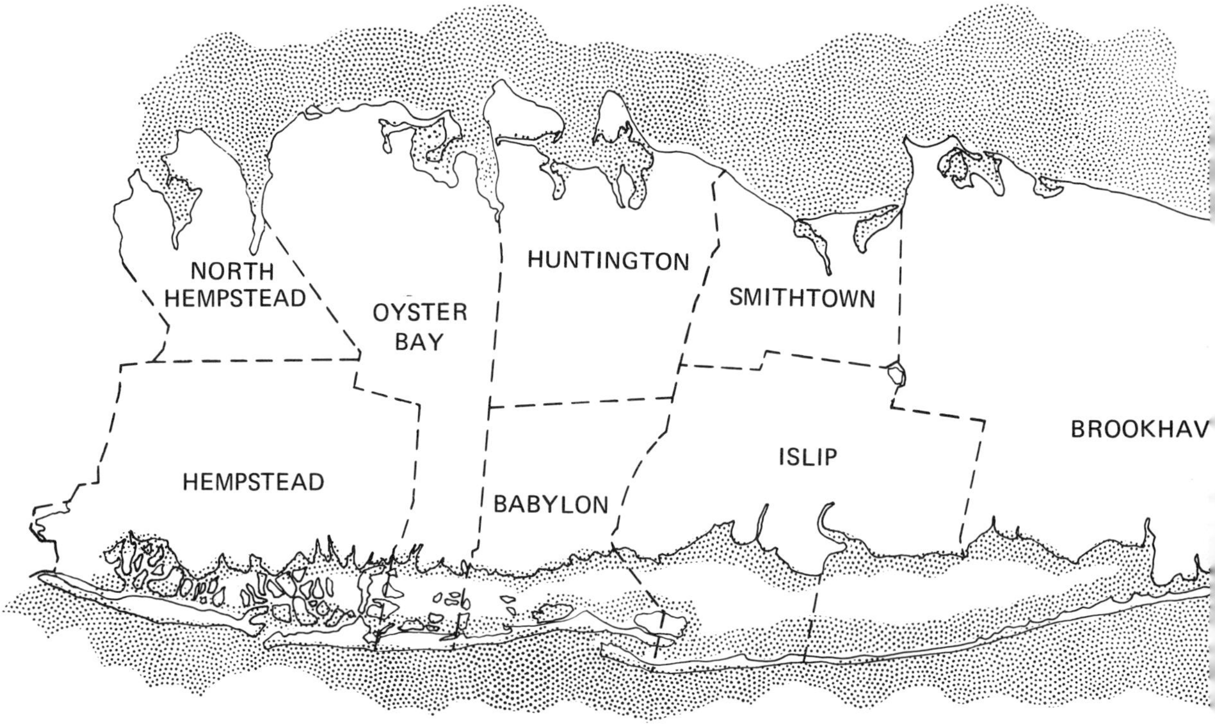
NORTH HEMPSTEAD
OYSTER BAY
HUNTINGTON
SMITHTOWN
HEMPSTEAD
BABYLON
ISLIP
BROOKHAV

L O N

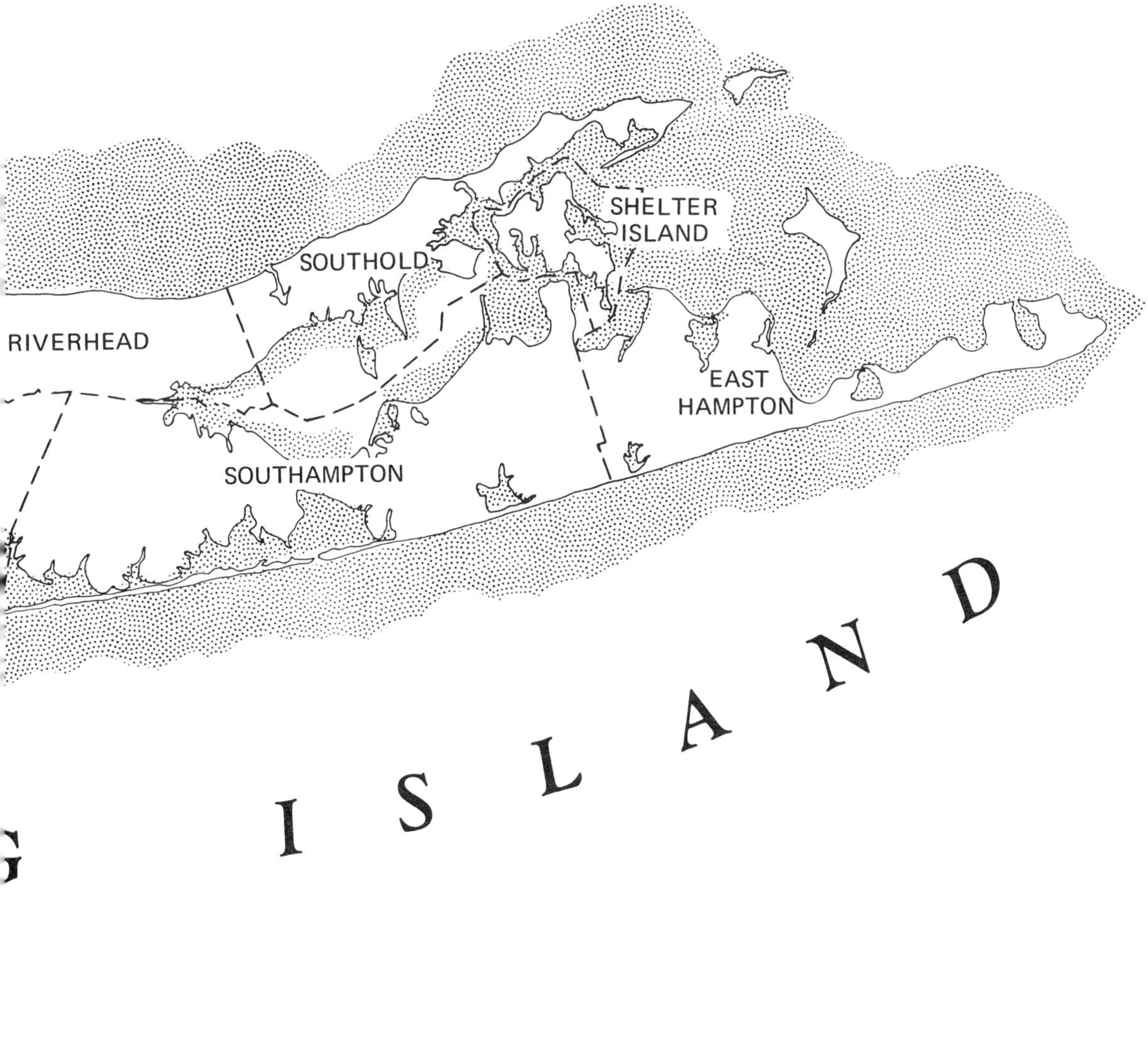
SHELTER
ISLAND
SOUTHOLD
RIVERHEAD
EAST
HAMPTON
SOUTHAMPTON
ISLAND

This report was prepared in the State Office of Planning Coordination's Metropolitan New York District Office, whose director is Howard S. Quinn. Staff participants were Edwin Friedman, Otto Mertz and Harold Kuplesky. The consultant was Edward J. Smits, and field surveys were made by two of his staff, Mrs. Harry R. Van Liew and Darrell D. Henning. Photographs are from Mr. Smits, Henry Eng, the Nassau County Historical Museum, the Brainard Collection and the State Department of Commerce. Permission has been granted to use several drawings from the *Cartoon History of Architecture* by Sir Osbert Lancaster, published by John Murray, Ltd., (pp. 10 and 11) from *College Hill* by the Providence (R. I.) City Plan Commission (doors on p. 8). The book was produced in OPC's Bureau of Communication, directed by John L. Moore. Design and layout were by Guy Brown and editing by Eleanor Billmyer.

As of April 1, 1971 the Office of Planning Coordination was superseded by the Office of Planning Services.